Contents

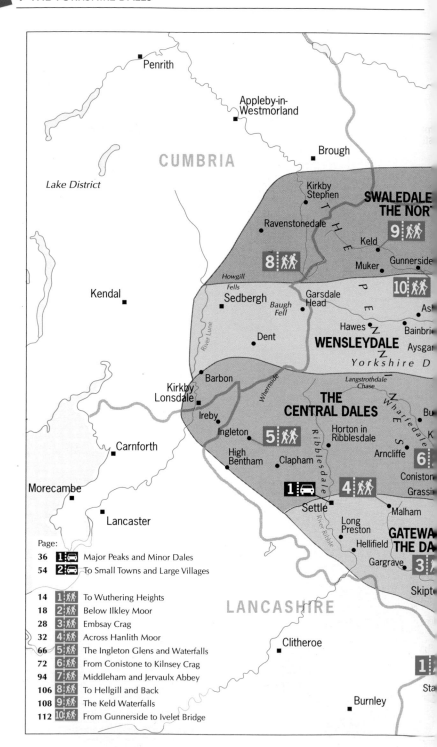

Penrith

Appleby-in-Westmorland

Brough

CUMBRIA

Lake District

Kirkby Stephen

SWALEDALE THE NOR

Ravenstonedale

Keld

9

Muker

Gunnerside

Howgill Fells

Sedbergh

Garsdale Head

10

Kendal

Baugh Fell

Hawes

Bainbri

Dent

WENSLEYDALE

Aysgar

River Lune

Yorkshire D

Barbon

Langstrothdale Chase

Kirkby Lonsdale

Whernside

THE CENTRAL DALES

Bu

Ireby

Wharfedale

K

Ingleton

Horton in Ribblesdale

Arncliffe

6

High Bentham

Clapham

Coniston

Carnforth

Ribblesdale

Grassi

Morecambe

4

Settle

GATEWA

Lancaster

Long Preston

Malham

THE DA

Hellifield

River Ribble

Gargrave

3

Skipt

LANCASHIRE

Clitheroe

1

Burnley

Sta

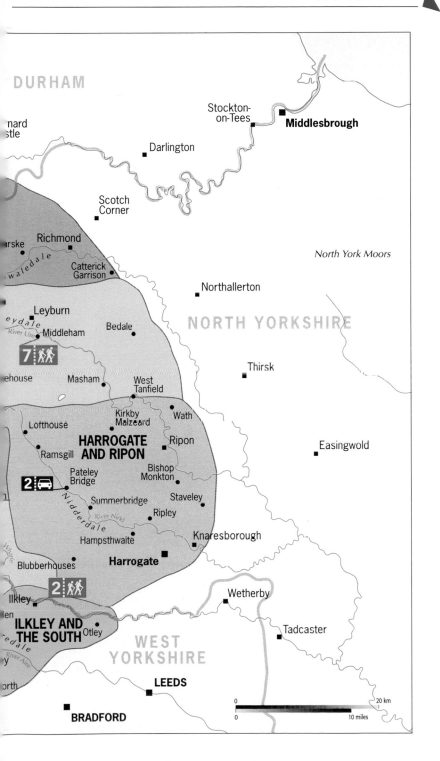

Introducing the Yorkshire Dales

The Yorkshire Dales is a land of hills and valleys, of waterfalls and rivers, of caves, country shows, and sheep on the hills. It is a landscape for walkers and artists, for those who love their food and drink and appreciate the hospitality of the friendly people who are lucky enough to live there.

Three hundred million years ago this area was beneath a tropical sea. As the creatures of the sea died, their bones and shells fell to the floor, gradually becoming compressed until they formed a block of limestone some 600 feet (183m) thick. As the earth's climate changed, pressure forced the limestone upwards into huge mounds and the seas drained.

Then the Ice Age came, and glaciers drove through the limestone to form gorges and valleys. When the ice receded, the landscape had been shaped, though later forests would grow and then die. Settlers moved in to farm the land, and today it is still farmed, though now ten million visitors also arrive each year to marvel at the area's beauty.

Right, neat meadows enclosed by drystone walls are characteristic of the rolling Yorkshire Dales

Above, water working against the limestone has shaped some of the most dramatic features of this landscape

Sheep are still the main livestock of the Dales; look out for sheepdog trials, left, and working dogs in the fields

Right, windowless stone barns scattered in the fields along each valley would have been used to store winter hay

Left, Thomas Chippendale, the famous furniture maker, was a son of the Dales, born and bred in Otley

THOMAS
CHIPPENDALE
world famous
CABINET MAKER
Born at OTLEY
1718

Right, this is the place to sample the light, crumbly cheese of Wensleydale – washed down perhaps with a spot of Theakston's Old Peculier ale

Visitors to the Wensleydale Creamery can learn more about the making of this local delicacy

The Dales provide excellent walking country, so take to the hills, above

THE TEN BEST LESSER-KNOWN DALES
Coverdale
Bishopdale
Littondale
Arkengarthdale
Widdale
Garsdale
Whitsundale
Colsterdale
Raydale
Little Dale

Above and left, the remarkable novels of the Brontës have brought the Yorkshire landscape to life for millions of readers around the world, and many enthusiasts follow the well-trodden path to the Brontë Parsonage Museum in Haworth

THE ESSENTIAL YORKSHIRE DALES
If you have limited time and you want to get to the heart of the Dales:

Climb one of the Three Peaks: Whernside, Pen-y-ghent or Ingleborough, or delve underground at the White Scar Caves... **See** the waterfalls at Aysgarth, Hardraw or Keld... **Walk** to Malham Cove, though not in high season... **Indulge** in afternoon tea at Betty's tea rooms in Harrogate... **Drive** along the high moorland road from Leyburn to Grinton, where James Herriot fell in love with the Dales... **Visit** one of the agricultural shows, or the Tuesday livestock market at Hawes... **Sample** Wensleydale cheese, washed down with a pint of Theakston's... **Treat yourself** to a meal at the justifiably popular Angel Inn at Hetton... **Discover** the history of the Dales at one of the excellent museums... **Contemplate** the tranquillity and grandeur of the ruins at Fountains Abbey... **Escape** to your own special dale, where you can find peace and make the place your own.

A Weekend in the Dales: Day One

For many of us a weekend or a long weekend is the most that can be managed as a break in busy lives. These four pages offer a loosely planned itinerary designed to ensure that you see and enjoy the very best of the area. Options for wet weather and children are given where possible. Places with Gazetteer entries are in **bold**.

Friday Night

Stay at the Devonshire Arms at **Bolton Abbey** – it has been voted the best hotel in Yorkshire on several occasions. An expensive treat.

Saturday Morning

Visit the magnificent ruins of Bolton Priory, beautifully set amidst woodland and pasture in a bend of the River Wharfe. Near by are the notorious rapids known as the Strid.

Drive north on the B6160 to **Grassington**, and take the B6265 east towards **Pateley Bridge**, passing Stump Cross Caverns, with their dramatic subterranean formations – an excellent option on a wet day. In Pateley Bridge itself is the delightful Nidderdale Museum, as well as craft and souvenir shops.

Stroll along the banks of the River Wharfe and visit the ancient priory of Bolton, above

Left, beware the rushing waters of the Strid in spate

Head for the delights of Pateley Bridge, left

Discover Switzerland in miniature at How Stean Gorge, left

Meditate in the monastic peace of Jervaulx, below

Saturday Lunch

A good choice for lunch is the Sportsman's Arms at Wath, in Nidderdale, just north of Pateley Bridge on the road towards Lofthouse. It is noted for its fish, and meals can be taken in the restaurant or the bar, with a stroll by the River Nidd to follow. Families might prefer to stay in Pateley Bridge, with its wide choice of pubs and cafés.

Saturday Afternoon

Continue north on the minor road towards Lofthouse, passing the Gouthwaite Reservoir, and follow the signs for the How Stean Gorge: Yorkshire's 'Little Switzerland'.

From Lofthouse head towards Masham, but just before the village of Healey take the Leyburn turning on your left, to bring you out on to the A6108 at **Jervaulx Abbey**. Head north west to **Middleham**, Yorkshire's smallest town, with tea shops, pubs, craft galleries and a chance to visit the ruins of Middleham Castle.

Saturday Night

The Miller's House Hotel is small and reasonably priced, but is very highly rated, especially for its fine food and wine. If it is full, Middleham has a host of guesthouse and pub accommodation.

Visit Middleham and its moody castle, right and below

A Weekend in the Dales: Day Two

Our second and final day in the Dales takes in the very best of the area. In the morning a riverside walk, followed by a drive to a series of waterfalls, and one of the Dales' prettiest villages. Take lunch in a 'Herriot' hotel, see where they make Wensleydale cheese, pass by the dramatic Three Peaks.

Sunday Morning

Early risers can watch Middleham's racehorses training on the gallops above the town. After breakfast, drive from Middleham via **Leyburn** on the A684 up Wensleydale, with short diversions to Aysgarth to see its triple falls, and to **West Burton**, a beautiful Dales village with one of the largest greens in the country. Continue on the A684, turning off into **Askrigg**, the heart of 'Herriot' country, where much of *All Creatures Great and Small* was filmed.

If the weather is wet, drive north from Leyburn on the A6108 to **Richmond**, with its castle and three contrasting museums. Return to the original route via the B6270 to Grinton and a minor road to **Castle Bolton** and then **Aysgarth Falls**.

Sunday Lunch

An ideal lunch spot is the King's Arms in Askrigg, with its old-fashioned back bar, filmed as the 'Drover's Arms' in *All Creatures Great and Small*, and a smart front bar serving better-than-average pub meals.

Left, don't miss the spectacular falls at Aysgarth

Visit Richmond's Norman castle, reflected, below, in the placid waters of the River Swale

Seek out the best locations at Askrigg, left

Sample the cheese of Wensleydale in Hawes, right

Sunday Afternoon

After lunch, head for **Hawes**, where the Wensleydale Creamery offers visitors a chance to watch the famous Wensleydale cheese being made, it also has its own museum and cheese shop. If time allows, the Dales Countryside Museum is in Hawes too, as well as a pottery and ropemaker.

Leave Hawes on the B6255 southwards for a lovely drive through a minor dale: Widdale. This is real dales walking country, as the Pennine Way runs parallel to the road, and both the Dales Way and the Ribble Way cross it.

Follow the Pennine Way to Pen-y-ghent, above, one of the Three Peaks

Ingleborough, left, is another of these famous peaks

Pull over when you reach the unmistakable Ribblehead Viaduct, and hope your visit coincides with a train crossing on its way between Settle and Carlisle. Beyond the viaduct you can see **Whernside**, the highest of the Dales' Three Peaks at 2,414 feet (736m). In late April you might see the fit fell runners competing in the annual Three Peaks Race.

The Shambles overlooks the Market Square in Settle

Turn left at the viaduct along the B6479 towards **Horton in Ribblesdale**, and you will pass between the other two peaks: **Pen-y-ghent** on your left, **Ingleborough** on your right. This road follows the River Ribble taking you down into **Settle**, where you might enjoy an afternoon tea at Ye Olde Naked Man Café before heading for home.

Ilkley and the South

This region may not be the 'real' Yorkshire Dales as we know them, but it does mark their start. Here the industrial regions of Yorkshire give way first to the moors around Haworth and Ilkley and then to the more open Dales landscape and the National Park to the north. It is an area which inspired the Brontës, which spawned the unofficial Yorkshire anthem (*On Ilkley Moor B'aht 'At*) and which provided the locations for *The Railway Children* and *Emmerdale*. Ilkley and Otley both stand in Wharfedale, while the River Aire runs by Haworth and Keighley on its journey eastwards from the Dales via Leeds to flow into the North Sea.

HAWORTH'S NAME
In the 13th century Haworth was known as Hauewrth, which derived from two Old English words, *haga* and *worth*, meaning hedge and enclosure respectively. Hence also the Worth Valley in which it stands.

HAWORTH West Yorkshire Map ref SE0337
Haworth owes its position as one of Britain's most popular tourist destinations not to its physical attraction but to a freak of fate. If the Reverend Patrick Brontë had not produced the literary offspring that he did, Haworth today would be an appealing but quiet town, noted for a steep cobbled street that leads up to its church, but no more. As it is, beyond the church is the Brontë Parsonage Museum, to which visitors flock from all round the world, while beyond on the moors, footpath signs in several languages direct thousands to the sites that inspired *Wuthering Heights*. (See Walk on page 14.)

The one-time home of Patrick Brontë and his children (Emily, Charlotte, Anne and Branwell) is now a museum in which their lives and literary works can be studied in equal detail. Manuscripts and paintings attract as much attention as their living rooms, or the room in which Emily Brontë died at the age of only 30. It is an interesting place to visit for anyone who has ever read *Wuthering Heights* or *Jane Eyre*, but it is advisable to avoid Bank Holidays and summer weekends when coach parties crowd the narrow corridors and block the doorways into the rooms. There is rather more space to browse in the modern extension which houses most of the literary artefacts.

Outside the Parsonage is the parish church, where all the Brontës except Anne are buried in the crypt. Aside from its Brontë connections, it is a striking church with appealing stained-glass windows and statuary. Other Brontë links in Haworth – discounting such places as the Brontë Garage – include the Black Bull Inn where Branwell drank, and the Old Apothecary where he bought his opium.

An earlier influence on the religious life of Haworth was John Wesley. He was a frequent visitor, and people would travel from as far away as Leeds to listen to him preach. His lengthy sermons would start at dawn and last all day, his chapel full to overflowing. Wesley inspired William Grimshaw, who subsequently spent 21 years as a Methodist minister in Haworth. Grimshaw's preaching became so renowned that his church had to be extended in order to house the full congregation, and by the time of his death in 1763 he was known throughout Britain.

Haworth itself is bulging with tea rooms and souvenir shops, and the tourist industry has meant that other attractions have grown up, including the Timmy Feather Exhibition. This is a reconstruction of one of Yorkshire's last handloom weaving workshops, the like of which were, at one time, the hub of industry in many northern towns. There are regular spinning and weaving demonstrations, and visitors have the opportunity to buy some of the goods in the shop.

At the foot of the very steep Main Street is Haworth's station on the Keighley and Worth Valley Railway line. Some of the line's old trains are on display here, but see Keighley on pages 20 and 21 for more information.

THE OXENHOPE STRAW RACE
One Sunday in each July, the village of Oxenhope near Haworth is transformed by this event, which goes back all the way to 1975. Rival teams compete to carry a bale of straw around the village, visiting – and drinking in – as many pubs as possible on the way. The race, which has a serious purpose in raising money for local hospitals, took off in a big way and now several hundred people take part (many in fancy dress) and several thousand watch them. There are various other activities over the whole weekend.

In its gloomy setting beside the graveyard of Haworth's church, the Brontë Parsonage is second only to Stratford as a place of literary pilgrimage

To Wuthering Heights

An easy walk over windswept moorlands to the atmospheric spot said to have inspired Emily Brontë's Wuthering Heights. Best in winter, when the Haworth tourists may be fewer and the scenery suitably bleak.

Time: 1½ hours. Distance: 4 miles (6.4km).
Location: 1 mile (1.6km) west of Haworth.
Start: From Haworth drive through Stanbury to the western outskirts of the village. On the left is a small island with a bus stop; drive up to the left where the narrow road widens to provide parking space. (OS grid ref: SE006369.)
OS Map: Outdoor Leisure 21 (South Pennines)
1:25,000.
See Key to Walks on page 121.

ROUTE DIRECTIONS

Follow the sign to Top Withins. Keep straight on, ignoring the road which branches off to the right, pass a building on the left, and keep to the right up a slight slope until you pass a cattle grid and reach a signpost. Take the right fork for Top Withins with **the moors** stretching away to your left. The path from here is straightforward, passing some houses on the right then continuing straight on in a long slow climb. Pass the remains of Lower Withins on the left and then continue on to the ruins of Top Withins.

At **Top Withins** take time to admire the view and soak up the atmosphere. Turn back to a signpost which directs you to the right, to the Brontë Waterfalls and Haworth. The path, very well-trodden from a million Brontë pilgrims, leads you down across a stream and up on the other side. Keep straight on, ignoring the footpath to the right signed to Haworth and Harbour Lodge.

Cross a stile and follow the path which now bears right (ignore the stile at the far left of this field). Go through a gate and follow the path which leads towards a derelict building before descending to the right towards the water and a kissing gate. Pass through the gate and from here you can see the **Brontë Waterfalls** ahead.

From the falls climb back up to the track and head for the derelict building. Two signposts, close to the building and to each other, send you in the direction of Stanbury. Cross a ladder stile and keep a fence on your left until you reach another signpost. Keep straight ahead for Stanbury. The path from here is quite obvious, with Lower Laithe Reservoir plainly visible in the distance on the right. The path brings you back up to the signpost just beyond the cattle grid where you previously followed the direction to Top Withins. This time turn right and head back to the car park.

POINTS OF INTEREST

The Moors
Emily Brontë described the moors that you see all around you as:
'A distant, dreamy, dim blue chain of mountains circling every side.'
This doesn't give a true impression of the nature of the moors which are, for most of the time, bleak, wet and windswept. Other places near by which have Brontë connections include Ponden Hall, which became Thrushcross Grange in *Wuthering Heights*, and Wycoller Hall, which Charlotte Brontë used as Ferndean Manor in *Jane Eyre*.

Top Withins
This now-derelict farmhouse has long been identified with the Wuthering Heights of Emily Brontë's novel, although the building, when it stood, bore no resemblance to that described in the book. A plaque at Top Withins bears this out and suggests that the author, inspired by the setting of Top Withins, placed her fictional Wuthering Heights here. It was certainly one of her favourite walks. Top Withins was an 'intake' farm, where the farmer would try to push back the wild moor to create more usable land, but since Top Withins fell into disuse the moor has slowly reclaimed its territory.

Brontë Waterfalls
Emily Brontë's favourite walk to Top Withins passes the Brontë Waterfalls, and it was to these falls that Charlotte Brontë took her very last walk. The falls are

long and narrow, perhaps somewhat disappointing to some, and in summer they can dry to just a trickle, but they are attractive in their own way, and not just to Brontë enthusiasts. The

The remote farmstead at Top Withins, inspiration for Emily Brontë

bridge was washed away in storms and had to be replaced in 1990.

B'AHT 'AT
Tradition has it that the words
to the unofficial Yorkshire
anthem, *On Ilkley Moor B'aht
'At*, were written by a church
choir from Halifax who were
having a picnic beneath the
Cow and Calf Rocks, on the
edge of Ilkley Moor. For non-
northerners, the title refers to
the inadvisability of venturing
out on to the moors without
(b'aht) a suitable head-
covering ('at).

*Ilkley is a genteel town in
the valley of the River
Wharfe*

ILKLEY West Yorkshire Map ref SE1147

Those who only know Ilkley through the renowned song
about Ilkley Moor might suppose that it is a heartily
northern place, full of cloth caps and people saying 'By
'eck'. In fact it's quite a 'posh' place, as former spa towns
tend to be. Antiques shops rub shoulders with expensive
dress shops, which attract customers from all over the
country, and in The Box Tree it has one of the best
restaurants in the north of England.

It is also well situated, with the heart of the Dales to
the north, easy access to Harrogate to the northeast and
Leeds to the southeast. The River Wharfe runs through
the town, and above it stands Ilkley Moor itself (see
Walk on page 18), where the original spa was located.
This is at the White Wells, cottages built in 1756 by the
local landowner, Squire Middleton. These surrounded
the spa and provided two plunge baths for visitors,
which were originally open-air but were later enclosed.
Ilkley's growth began with the discovery of these mineral
springs, whose particularly cold nature was believed to
enhance their curative effects. Today the cottages
contain a small museum, with displays about the
Victorian spas as well as local wildlife and walks.
Opening hours are limited, though.

As the railway reached Ilkley in 1865, it brought
regular visitors to such an extent that by the end of the
century there were no less than 15 springs open to the
public. The railways also brought wealth to the town
with the arrival of industrialists from Bradford and
Leeds, keen to find somewhere more pleasant to live. As
a result, Ilkley now boasts some handsome Victorian
architecture, with arcades of shops as well as more
modern shopping precincts.

On Ilkley Moor, near the White Wells, are the dramatic Cow and Calf Rocks, and even if you lack the time or the inclination to venture on to the moor itself, you should try to see these striking features. Ilkley Moor is a part of the larger Rombald's Moor, and Rombald was a local giant whose name crops up here and there in the region. He once chased his wife across Ilkley Moor and tripped over the large Cow Rock, chipping off a chunk which landed near by to form the Calf Rock. Local climbers practice on these sheer surfaces.

In the centre of town is the parish church of All Saints, well worth a visit for its Saxon crosses, two Roman altars and splendid stained glass, some designed by the William Morris Gallery. A Burne-Jones window can be seen in St Margaret's Church, built in 1879 and located in Queens Road. In the gardens opposite is the Panorama Stone, the most accessible of the several prehistoric carved rocks in and around Ilkley.

Next to All Saints Church is the Manor House Museum. This is believed to stand on the site of the Roman fort of Olicana, built in AD 79, which later appeared in the Domesday Book as Illiclei. The Museum has a small collection, and includes a gallery where temporary modern exhibitions are displayed. It is not known whether the Manor House was the vicarage for All Saints or whether it might have been a yeoman farmer's house. Whichever it was, an unusual feature is its 17th-century wall privy.

Generations have left their mark on the Cow and Calf rocks above the town

DARWIN GARDENS AND THE ORIGIN OF SPECIES

In 1859, Charles Darwin published *On the Origin of Species* and took refuge in the spa facilities at Ilkley as the repercussions began to materialise. Initially staying in Wells House, he was joined by his family and moved to North View House, now incorporated into the large building on the left at the top of Wells Road. To celebrate Ilkley's connections with the pioneering evolutionist, the former pleasure gardens across the road have been transformed into a Millennium Green known as Darwin Gardens with a maze, several monuments and rejuvenated paths and woodland.

Below Ilkley Moor

A long but straightforward walk on the edge of Ilkley Moor, giving glorious views of Wharfedale. Best in summer, for the superb views.

Time: 3 hours. Distance: 6½ miles (10.4km).
Location: Ilkley.
Start: Park in the car park at Darwin Gardens at the top of Wells Road. (OS grid ref: SE117471.)
OS Map: Explorer 297 (Lower Wharfedale & Washburn Valley) 1:25,000.
See Key to Walks on page 121.

ROUTE DIRECTIONS

From the car park turn right, pass Wells House and turn left into a road signed 'No Through Road'. Take the path which leads off to the right before the stone bridge. Cross the footbridge, pass behind houses to your right, then pass a reservoir. Take the path which leads off to the left about 10 yards (3m) before the footbridge over a stream. The path crosses the same stream a little higher up; continue and pass through a fallen-down wall towards the fence around the **Swastika Stone**.

The path is now well-defined and easy to follow and skirts the edge of the moor. Continue for 1½ miles (2.4km), crossing many stiles. Turn right on to the path marked by a pile of stones and pass through a gap in the rocks known as Windgate Nick. The path now divides; take the right fork and follow it down to a stile. Go over the stile and continue down the next field until you reach a wall that comes in from the left. Follow the wall down to a stile, go over the stile putting the wall on your right and

follow this to reach a lane.

Cross the lane, go through a gate, following the road to a cattle grid where a footpath sign on your left directs you to a stile. Over this, the path heads down through several fields. In the first, make for the right of a broken wall, turning left when it turns left. Turn right around some trees, keeping the wire fence on your left. You reach a stile in

the bottom wall. Keep to the left over two more stiles, before veering right to a third stile in the far corner of the field. Don't cross the footbridge, but climb the stone stile in front of you. The path rises to cross a field, then drops to cross a narrow stream. Veer left and walk ahead near the trees at the edge of the field to a gate which takes you to the right of a house, on to the access road for this farm. Follow this down to the main road.

Turn right to the A65. Cross straight over the road to a path that leads right, down to the next side road. Cross this and head left, to a footpath sign that sends you right. This is the **Dales Way** which goes back to Ilkley. It is easy to follow, but watch for a footbridge on your left, which leads you behind a white house. The path is well-walked and takes you over numerous stiles until it emerges at the Tennis Club.

Turn right along the entrance road and where this swings right, go straight ahead along the footpath to **Ilkley Bridge**, an old stone bridge. Cross the road, staying on the same side of the river, go down some steps and on to the next bridge. Steps take you up to the main road. Turn right and walk ahead up through **Ilkley** to the car park.

POINTS OF INTEREST

The Swastika Stone
One of only three such stones known to exist in the world, and the only one in Britain, the Swastika Stone dates from prehistoric times and was believed to have been used by fire-worshippers.

The Dales Way
This long-distance footpath, set up in 1968, starts in Ilkley and runs for a distance of 84 miles (135km), mostly along the River Wharfe in the early stages, until it reaches

Bowness on the shores of Windermere in Cumbria.

Ilkley Bridge
The low parapets on this old packhorse bridge were built this way in order to prevent the loads that were being carried by the packhorses from banging against the side of the bridge and being damaged.

Climbers train on the steep crags of the Cow and Calf

Ilkley
Ilkley was a popular spa town in Victorian times, and the springs at White Wells on the moor are now restored. Ilkley has a museum and several old churches and is noted particularly for its shopping.

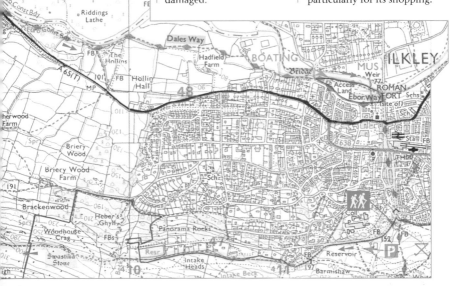

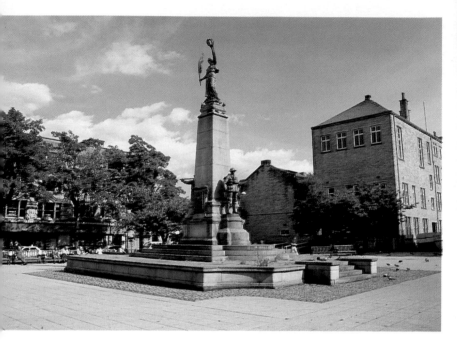

An impressive war memorial stands in the square of the prosperous mill town of Keighley

KEIGHLEY'S WILDLIFE
Known as a northern industrial town which expanded due to the Industrial Revolution, Keighley still harbours a great deal of the wildlife that lived here before the looms and mills came along. The local Naturalists' Society has devised a 2-mile (3.2-km) walk which incorporates a stretch of the Leeds–Liverpool Canal and the industrial heartland of the town, where visitors are reminded that they are still in Airedale by the presence of rabbits, foxes and the occasional badger. Details of the walk can be obtained from the Haworth Tourist Information Centre, as Keighley does not have a Centre of its own.

KEIGHLEY West Yorkshire Map ref SE0541
Although only about 3 miles (4.8km) north of Haworth off the A629, Keighley is a world away for the average visitor. Brontë pilgrims from America and Japan may flock to Haworth Parsonage – the home of the close-knit Brontë family, now a museum with displays of personal memorabilia – but few have probably even heard of this northern mill town which, nevertheless, has plenty to offer the visitor.

Shoppers should note that as well as the large modern Airedale Shopping Centre with its selection of major department stores, Keighley has several of the north's traditional mill shops, through which factories would at one time sell their own goods to workers at reduced prices. These are now more commercial operations and sell a wide variety of goods, especially footwear, clothing, bedding and woollens.

Haworth and Keighley are linked by the Keighley and Worth Valley Railway, a 5-mile (8-km) stretch of branch line, run by enthusiasts, which links with the Leeds–Settle–Carlisle main line at Keighley Station: platforms 1 and 2 are the main line, 3 and 4 the Keighley and Worth Valley Railway. The line was built mainly to serve the valley's mills, and runs through the heart of Brontë country. At the station the concourse and booking hall have been beautifully restored to their late 19th-century splendour, complete with a glass canopy, and there is also a locomotive turntable on display, but the main attractions require a trip on the train. The first stop down the line is Ingrow West; here you will find the Vintage Railway Carriage Museum, where visitors can watch the restoration work taking place, and the Bahamas Locomotive Society collection of steam locomotives.

The next stop is the gas-lit Damems Station, the smallest fully-operational station in Britain, but a request stop only. Oakworth Station has also been restored in Edwardian fashion, complete with gas lamps and old tin advertisement signs. It may look familiar to anyone who has seen the film, *The Railway Children*. Haworth Station is next, and finally Oxenhope, where the main Railway Museum is situated and where there is also a buffet restaurant. The museum has a large collection of trains and carriages, including royal carriages and the train used in *The Railway Children*. There are also two tunnels along the line, and a good day out can be had by travelling the full length of it, stopping off at each station on the way. A journey along the line without stopping would take about 25 minutes. The railway organises a popular programme of events for families and enthusiasts alike, including Thomas the Tank Engine weekends and Santa Specials.

The first stop in Keighley should be the Cliffe Castle Museum, a 19th-century mansion northwest of the town on the A629. The museum specialises in the geology and natural history of the region and has hands-on opportunities as well as touring exhibitions. One popular exhibit is a model of a giant newt which used to live in the area. There are also Victorian toys, general local historical items and a working beehive, the bees coming in and out through a tube which leads to a hole in the wall.

THE AIREDALE HEIFER
This enormous animal was kept at East Riddlesden Hall in the 19th century and achieved fame throughout the Dales because of its size – it was almost 12 feet (3.6m) long. When finally slaughtered in 1830 it was found to weigh one and a quarter tons (1,270kg).

Oxenhope is one of six stations along the 4¾-mile Keighley and Worth Valley Railway

EMMERDALE

The TV soap set in the Dales draws on a variety of local places for its inspiration. Otley becomes Hotten, with its market, and the opening titles flash through a dizzying mix of mostly Wharfedale landscapes. Although originally made in Arncliffe in Littondale, until a few years ago the exterior shots for Emmerdale were filmed on location in the the village of Esholt, between Leeds and Bradford. Now there is a purpose-built set in the grounds of Harewood House. Sadly this isn't open to the public, but Esholt makes a worthy trip for true fans. You can still tour the interior sets for the series at weekends and even have a pint in the Woolpack. They are in the unDaleslike backlots of Yorkshire TV studios on Burley Road in Leeds. Call Emmerdale Tours (01274 562107) for further details.

Fragments of a Viking tombstone in Otley parish church confirm that this part of Wharfedale has been occupied for centuries

Rather less brash is the National Trust's East Riddlesden Hall, one mile (1.6km) northeast of the town on the Bradford Road. This 17th-century Yorkshire manor house is set in 12 acres (4.9ha) of land with attractive gardens, a duck pond and a particularly fine medieval tithe barn which houses a collection of old agricultural implements. The gardens include a monastic fishpond and a restored walled garden. Inside the Hall itself are mullioned windows, panelled rooms and collections of furniture, pewter, embroidery and kitchen utensils, as well as the impressive original kitchen and plenty of ghost stories from the helpful attendants.

OTLEY West Yorkshire Map ref SE2045

When the television series *Emmerdale* wanted a town that could give them a bustling livestock market for filming, they chose Otley in Lower Wharfedale. The town has had a market since Saxon times, and the first market charter was granted in 1222. There are cattle markets on Monday and Friday, with general street markets on Friday and Saturday (Tuesday as well during the summer months). Otley can also boast one of the oldest agricultural shows in the country, dating back to 1796. At first just a cattle show, today it is a highlight of the Otley calendar and includes rare breeds and the splendid Shire horses.

Otley's parish church of All Saints has some Anglian crosses which date from AD 750, an early 14th-century tower, a Norman doorway and some lovely Victorian stained-glass windows, though the town's main attraction is simply itself. It is a busy working town, but with attractive 17th- and 18th-century buildings and streets with ancient names, such as Kirkgate, Bondgate and Boroughgate.

Thomas Chippendale, 1718–79, one of the most celebrated cabinet makers and designers that the world has ever known, was born in Otley, where his family were joiners and where he served his own apprenticeship, probably at a shop in Boroughgate.

Ilkley and The South

Leisure Information

Places of Interest

Shopping

The Performing Arts

Sports, Activities
and the Outdoors

Annual Events and Customs

Checklist ✔

Leisure Information

TOURIST INFORMATION CENTRES

Haworth
2-4 West Lane. Tel: 01535
642329.
Ilkley
Station Road. Tel: 01943
602319.
Otley
4 Boroughgate. Tel: 0113 247
7707.

OTHER INFORMATION

**British Waterways Board
Headquarters**
Willow Grange, Church Road,
Watford. Tel: 01923 226422.
www.british-waterways.org
English Heritage
37 Tanner Row, York. Tel: 01904
601901.
www.english-heritage.org.uk
Environment Agency
21 Park Square South, Leeds.
Tel: 0113 244 0191.
National Trust
Yorkshire Regional Office
Goddards, 27 Tadcaster Road,
Dringhouses, York.
Tel: 01904 702021.
www.nationaltrust.org.uk
RSPB
www.rspb.com

**Yorkshire Dales National
Park Authority**
www.yorkshiredales.org.uk
Yorkshire Museums Council
www.yorkshiremuseums.org.uk
Yorkshire Tourist Board
www.ytb.org.uk
Yorkshire Wildlife Trust
10 Toft Green, York. Tel: 01904
659570. www.yorkshire-wildlife-
trust.org.uk

ORDNANCE SURVEY MAPS

Landranger 1:50,000 Sheet 104.
Outdoor Leisure 1:25,000 Sheet
21. Explorer 1:25,000 Sheet 27.

Places of Interest

There will be an admission
charge at the following places of
interest unless otherwise stated.
Brontë Parsonage Museum
Church Street. Haworth.Tel:
01535 642323. Open all year,
except mid-Jan to mid-Feb and
Christmas.
**Cliffe Castle Museum and
Gallery**
Spring Gardens Lane, Keighley.
Tel: 01535 618230. Open all
year, closed Mon. Free.
East Riddlesden Hall
Bradford Road, Keighley.Tel:
01535 607075. Manor house

and tithe barn. Open Apr–Oct,
certain days.
**Keighley and Worth Valley
Railway**
Haworth. Tel: 01535 647777
(timetable) or 01535 645214
(enquiries). Stations at Keighley,
Haworth, Oxenhope, and
Ingrow West. Steam and diesel
engines. Services: weekends all
year, also Bank Hols and daily
Jul–early Sep; special events.
**Manor House Gallery and
Museum**
Castle Yard, Church Street,
Ilkley. Tel: 01943 600066. Open
all year, closed Mon and Tue.
Otley Museum
Civic Centre, Boroughgate,
Otley. Tel: 01943 461052.
Modest collection of printing
machinery. Open all year, Mon,
Tue, Fri morning and 1st Sat of
month. Closed 25–26 Dec.
Railway Carriage Museum
Ingrow Railway Centre,
Keighley. Tel: 01535 680425.
Open all year, most days.
Timmy Feather Exhibition
Brontë Weaving Shed, Townend
Mill, Haworth. Tel: 01535
646217. Workshop of the last
handloom weaver in Yorkshire;
demonstrations of weaving and
spinning at weekends and some

days in summer. Open all year, most days. Free.

White Wells Spa Cottage
Access from Wells Road, Ilkley. Tel: 01943 608035. Museum within the original spa, stone plunge pool and displays on Victorian ailments and cures. Café. Open all year, weekends, most BHs. Some weekdays in summer as indicated by flags flying outside.

SPECIAL INTEREST FOR CHILDREN

The following places may be of interest to visitors with children.

The Black Bull inn at the top of Haworth's steep high street has a reputation for good food

Unless stated there will be an admission charge.

Keighley and Worth Valley Railway
Haworth. Tel: 01535 647777 (timetable) or 01535 645214 (enquiries). There are stations at Keighley, Haworth, Oxenhope, and Ingrow West.
Steam and diesel engines run through Brontë country. Services operate weekends all year, also Bank Hols and daily Jul–early Sep; special events.

Railway Carriage Museum
Ingrow Railway Centre, Keighley.
Tel: 01535 680425. Open all year, most days. Closed 25–26 Dec.

Timmy Feather Exhibition
Brontë Weaving Shed, Townend Mill, Haworth.Tel: 01535 646217. The workshop of the

last handloom weaver in Yorkshire; there are demonstrations of weaving and spinning at weekends and some days in summer. Open all year, most days.

Shopping

Ilkley
The main shopping areas are: Brook Street, The Grove, Victorian Arcade. Around the main car park there are shops on the Grove Promenade and in a small shopping centre. There is a range of specialist shops including delicatessens, books, fashion and antiques.

Keighley
The Airedale Centre is a large shopping complex with many major department stores. An indoor market is open

Mon–Sat (except Tue pm).
There is a factory shop in
Lawkholme Lane.
Otley
Open-air market Tue, Fri and Sat
all year. Livestock markets held
Mon.

LOCAL SPECIALITIES

Mill Shops
Ponden Mill, Colne Rd,
Stanbury.
Tel: 01535 643500.
A large complex in an 18th-
century mill, with crafts, gifts,
linen and clothing.
Brontë Weaving Shed, North
Street, Haworth. Tel: 01535
646217. Open all year daily.
Clothing and gifts.
**Prints, Paintings and
Pottery**
The Gascoigne Gallery, 122
Bolling Road, Ben Rhydding,
Ilkley.
Tel: 01943 600725.

The Performing Arts

Ilkley Playhouse
Weston Road, Ilkley.
Tel: 01943 609539.
Keighley Playhouse
Devonshire Street, Keighley.
Tel: 01535 601764.
King's Hall Complex
Station Road, Ilkley.
Tel: 01274 751576.
Victoria Hall
Victoria Park, Hard Ings Road,
Keighley.
Tel: 01535 681763 ext 228.

Sports, Activities and the Outdoors

ANGLING

Fly
Ilkley Sections of the River
Wharfe: daily or weekly permits
are available from Ilkley Tourist
Information Centre.
Tel: 01943 602319.
Coarse
Keighley Leeds–Liverpool Canal
and along the River Aire.
Permits are available from:
K L Tackle, 127 North Street.
Tel: 01535 667574
Willis Walker (Sports),
105–109 Cavendish Street.
Tel: 01535 602928

CANOEING

Haworth
Ponden Reservoir: contact
Ponden Boat Users Association.
Tel: 01535 643367.

CLIMBING

Ilkley
Popular at Cow and Calf Rocks,
on edge of Ilkley Moor.
Permission not needed.

COUNTRY PARKS, WOODS AND NATURE RESERVES

Middleton Woods, near Ilkley.

GOLF COURSES

Ilkley
Ben Rhydding Golf Club, High
Wood, Ben Rhydding.
Tel: 01943 608759.
Ilkley Golf Club, Nesfield Road,
Middleton. Tel: 01943 600214.
Keighley
Branshaw Golf Club, Branshaw
Moor, Oakworth.
Tel: 01535 643235.
Keighley Golf Club, Howden
Park, Utley. Tel: 01535 604778.

HORSE-RIDING

Keighley
Truewell Hall Riding Centre,
Holme House Lane, Goose Eye.
Tel: 01535 603792.

LONG-DISTANCE FOOTPATHS AND TRAILS

The Abbots Hike
A 79-mile (127-km) walk
through the Yorkshire Dales
National Park and across the
Pennines from Ilkley to Pooley
Bridge in the Lake District
National Park.
The Dales Way
A 81-mile (130-km) walk from
Ilkley to Bowness on
Windermere. The Dales Way
links the Yorkshire Dales
National Park with the Lake
District National Park.

ORIENTEERING

Ilkley
There are permanent
orienteering courses on Ilkley
Moor and in Middleton Woods.
For further information contact
Ilkley Tourist Informaiton Centre,
Station Road.
Tel: 01943 602319.

RUGBY

Keighley
Keighley Cougars Rugby League
Football Club, Cougar Park,
Royd Ings Avenue.
Tel: 01535 213111.
Otley
Otley Rugby Union Football
Club, Cross Green.
Tel: 01943 461180.

WATERSPORTS

Haworth
Ponden Reservoir. (Canoeing,
windsurfing). For information
contact Ponden Boat Users
Association. Tel: 01535 643367.

Annual Events and Customs

Haworth
Oxenhope Straw Race, July.
Ilkley
Ilkley Carnival, May Day Bank
Holiday.
Literature Festival, once or twice
a year, Contact the Festival
Office on Tel: 01943 601210.
Wharfedale Music Festival, week-
long event, starts two weeks
before Spring Bank Holiday.
Otley
Otley Show, Saturday before
Spring Bank Holiday.
Otley Carnival, late June.
Christmas Victorian Fair,
December.

The checklists give details of just
some of the facilities within the
area covered by this guide.
Further information can be
obtained from Tourist
Information Centres.

Gateway to the Dales

Skipton is the main claimant to the title of 'Gateway to the Dales', and it is the principal town on the A65 that runs along the southern boundary of the National Park and links the M1 and the M6. In fact, the road bypasses most of the interesting small towns alongside it, such as Settle and Giggleswick, and has delightful views of the hills to the north and, for much of the way, valleys and green fields dropping away to the south. Skipton also gives easy access to the most popular place in the whole National Park – Malham – and the varied attractions of the Bolton Abbey Estate.

WORDSWORTH'S WHITE DOE

In 1807 William Wordsworth toured the area near Bolton Priory, and heard the local legend which he then retold in his poem, *The White Doe of Rylstone*, published in 1815. Set in the early 16th century, it tells the tale of the Norton family: Francis gives a white doe to his sister, Emily, before going off to fight in a rebellion. He survives the rebellion but is murdered in Norton Tower on his return home. During her despair, Emily is comforted by the same white doe that returns from the wild, and it accompanies her on her visits to her brother's grave. Long after Emily's death, the white doe can still be seen lying on Francis's grave.

BOLTON ABBEY   North Yorkshire Map ref SE0754

The Bolton Abbey Estate, which is owned by the Duke and Duchess of Devonshire, is an enjoyable amalgamation of the recreational, the historical and the geographical – not to mention the hedonistic, with guests at the Devonshire Arms enjoying one of the best hotels in the country, and one of the region's best restaurants. For most people, though, Bolton Abbey is a day out in the car, within easy reach of the cities of Bradford and Leeds, with ample parking and plenty to see and do.

The first people to enjoy the site, if not quite the present facilities, were the Augustinian monks who moved here from Embsay in 1154 to found a new priory, which was finished by the following century and now lies in evocative ruins in a meadow by the banks of the River Wharfe. The adjoining priory church of Saint Mary and Saint Cuthbert is far from being in ruins, though, and is one of the finest churches in the Dales. First built in 1220, it escaped the destruction of Henry VIII's Dissolution of the Monasteries, only to fall victim to dwindling congregations in the 1970s. Now magnificently restored, it has breathtaking stained glass and wall paintings.

If you drive along the B6160 to one of the several car parks (day tickets allow you to move from one car park to another to explore the estate fully) you will pass under a narrow stone archway, part of an aqueduct which once carried water to the mill of which little now remains. There are several shops on the estate selling Bolton Abbey branded goods, as well as restaurants and a pub, many of them part of the village of Bolton Abbey, which grew up beside the priory.

Although it is possible to stroll around and do nothing very energetic, there are also good walks to be had around the estate, including several marked nature trails near the river and through Strid Wood, which is a Site of Special Scientific Interest. A leaflet showing the colour-coded walks is handed to visitors at the car park entrance. There are over 60 different varieties of plants and about 40 species of birds nest there every year. Spring brings snowdrops and later whole rivers of bluebells, and in summer the air is thick with dragonflies, butterflies and bees. Local nature groups post notices letting the visitors know what they are likely to see at the time of their visit.

A few miles north of Bolton Abbey on the B6160 are the imposing ruins of Barden Tower, built in 1485 and home to Henry, Lord Clifford, who was known as the Shepherd Lord because he was raised as a shepherd. The tower was repaired by Lady Anne Clifford in the 17th century, but later fell into disuse, although it remains an atmospheric site.

THE STRID

As it flows through the Bolton Abbey Estate in one place the River Wharfe thunders through a narrow ravine just a few feet across – little more than a stride, or strid. If you feel a desire to jump across, bear in mind that several people have been killed as they slipped on the rocks and fell into the fast-flowing river, which is up to 30 feet (9m) deep in places. One of the leaflets handed to visitors asks them to 'remember that anything that goes into the Strid rarely surfaces for several days'. Be warned!

The ruins of Bolton Abbey lie in a spectacularly lovely riverside setting

Embsay Crag

A fairly easy walk over farmland and by a reservoir with beautiful views of Embsay Crag. Best walked in the summer in dry weather. The path up to Embsay Crag adds an extra half an hour and half a mile to the walk.

Time: 1½ hours. Distance: 3 miles (4.8km).
Location: 2 miles (3.2km) north of Skipton off the A65.
Start: Park in the free car park in the centre of Embsay village.
(OS grid ref: SE009538.)
OS Map: Outdoor Leisure 2
(Yorkshire Dales – Southern & Western areas)
1:25,000.
See Key to Walks on page 121.

ROUTE DIRECTIONS

Leave by the gate at the back of the car park in **Embsay**, turn left and walk diagonally across the field to the stone steps in the wall. Cross the next field heading to the right of the school fence and walk with the school on your left. More steps take you out of this field. Cross a farm track and go over a stile to another stone stile in the bottom left corner of the field. The footpath is well signposted along this section of the walk. Turn slightly to the right to cross the next field, passing behind the houses. Cross two more fields, always heading to the far left corners, until you reach the minor road which leads up to Embsay Moor Reservoir, which is on the right. Pass the footpath sign on the left to 'None-Go-Bye', a farm about 2 miles (3.2km) west of the reservoir.

Continue on this quiet road, which eventually bears left and becomes a bridleway to Embsay Kirk and Embsay Crag. Continue and pass the Craven Sailing Club at Embsay Reservoir on the right. Ignore the first footpath sign and follow the second sign on the right signed 'Embsay Crag', which now stands imposingly before you. Cross the stile and follow the path, which veers right after about 100 yards (91m), keeping close to the reservoir wall which is on your right. Cross the wooden bridge over the beck that flows into the reservoir. The path up to **Embsay Crag** leads off to the left, and adds about half a mile (800m) and half an hour to the walk.

Continue ahead on the path which hugs the reservoir wall and rises slowly to pass in front of Embsay Crag. Here it passes through ferns from which startled rabbits may run as you approach. Pass behind Grouse Cottage on your right and continue ahead.

Turn right on to the path signed 'Footpath and Bridleway to Eastby'. Go through the gate, down through several fields and pass a farm where the path becomes an asphalt track. Follow it down to the left, over a cattle grid, and turn right at the road. Walk along the road as it bears sharp left and passes the Church of St Mary the Virgin, where a footpath sign on the right directs you across another field and back to the stile at the rear of the car park. Visit the **Embsay and Bolton Abbey Steam Railway** in the village if you have time.

POINTS OF INTEREST

Embsay
An Augustinian Priory was founded here in 1130, but the monks found the life very difficult at Embsay and moved in 1154 to what is now Bolton Priory, taking the path across Embsay Moor. A Bronze-Age settlement at Embsay is marked by a stone circle found near the village.

Embsay Crag
Standing 1,217 feet (371m) high, Embsay Crag faces south with views across to the strangely shaped Haw Park Hill – its straight sides are a result of extensive quarrying. Behind the Crag to the north lies Embsay Moor, climbing up to over 1,312 feet (400m). Walkers need to take care around the old coal pits and disused shafts found here.

Embsay and Bolton Abbey Steam Railway
The steam railway, based at Embsay Station, was opened in 1888 by the Midland Railway to link Ilkley with Skipton and the through route to Carlisle and Scotland. It now houses a café and a large railway

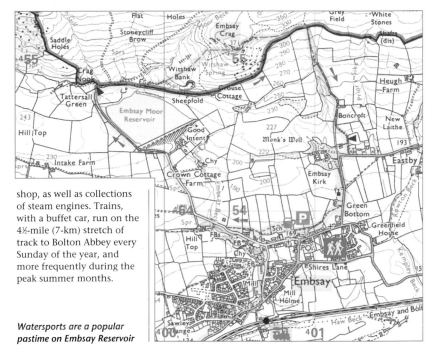

shop, as well as collections of steam engines. Trains, with a buffet car, run on the 4½-mile (7-km) stretch of track to Bolton Abbey every Sunday of the year, and more frequently during the peak summer months.

Watersports are a popular pastime on Embsay Reservoir

THE QUAKERS

Airton, near Malham, is one of the largest villages in the Dales without a pub. This is due to the influence of the Quakers in the 16th and 17th centuries, among whom the drinking of alcohol was strictly forbidden. Visitors will have to seek spiritual refreshment by visiting the Friends Meeting House instead. This was founded by William and Alice Ellis, whose own house can still be seen with their initials above the door.

THE AIRTON SQUATTERS

Airton has a squatter's cottage, on the green. It was built in the 17th century when the law stated that if a person could build a home and have smoke rising from its chimney within 24 hours, they were entitled to the freehold of the property for a distance as far as a stone could be thrown from the front door.

The Malham Landscape Trail is just one route for exploring Malham Cove

MALHAM North Yorkshire Map ref SD9063

Malham is a magnet for visitors to the Dales. Malham Cove is one of Britain's most impressive natural features and consequently the area has become almost too popular for its own good. At busy times the National Park Centre car park overflows and the roadside verges disappear under the wheels of parked cars. The village streets give off a heady scent of cagoules and Kendal mint cake, and there are a number of cafés, pubs, outdoor shops and guesthouses to accommodate the crowds. It is a place to visit, certainly, but choose when you go.

The half-mile (800m) walk to Malham Cove is signed from the village centre and should not be missed. The name Malham Cove is a mix of Old Scandinavian and Old English words, which provide a suitably mythological-sounding description of it: 'The secluded cavern by the gravelly places'. The limestone rock face seems to tumble down the 250-foot (76m) cliffs, and extends for about 1,000 feet (305m). Try to picture the water that once flowed over the cliff face, helping create today what has been aptly described as a 'dry waterfall'. This natural amphitheatre was formed by movements of the earth's crust, and is simply the most visible part of the Craven Fault, which runs through this district of Craven. It is a steep climb up man-made steps to the top, but the reward is an exhilarating view over the moors around Malham, north to Malham Tarn and especially over the strange limestone pavements which stretch away from beneath your feet. The limestone slabs are known as clints, while the gaps between them are grikes, and it is in these grikes that some of the area's wide variety of unusual plants can be found.

Malham Tarn, to the north of the village, is in the care of the National Trust and the Field Studies Council. At about 150 acres (61ha), it is slightly smaller than Semer Water (see page 98), but can claim to be the highest natural lake in the Pennines. Malham Tarn is 1,229 feet (374m) above sea level, and both the tarn and the area around it have been declared a Site of Special Scientific Interest. A track leads down past Tarn House, where the Field Studies Council run regular courses on the natural history of the area. It is especially important for plant life and as a breeding area for many birds: a hide is open to the public to enable views of parts of the lake which cannot be accessed on foot. Tarn House, a former shooting lodge, was also the home of Walter Morrison whose visitors at various times included Charles Darwin, John Ruskin and Charles Kingsley. It was while staying at Tarn House that Kingsley was inspired to write his children's classic, *The Water Babies*.

Malham's other natural attractions include Gordale Scar and Janet's Foss, both covered in our Walk on page 32, while the village of Kirkby Malham, a little way to the south, is also of interest. Its name derives from the time of the Danes, Kirkby being a village with a church, near to Malham. The church has many notable features, but one of the most significant is certainly one of the three bells. It was cast in 1601 and weighs one and a quarter tons, making it the second largest bell in Britain.

The Field Studies Centre at Malham Tarn provides residential space for students of all ages to learn about the area

THE BRIDGES OF MALHAM

In their haste to see Malham Cove, many visitors overlook the two old bridges in the village centre. The New Bridge, as it is known, is also called the Monks' Bridge and was built in the 17th century, then widened in the 18th. It can be seen near the post office. Malham's older bridge dates from the 16th century and is of clapper design, with large slabs of limestone placed on stone supports in the stream. This is the Wash-Dub or Moon Bridge, named after Prior Moon, the last Prior of Bolton Abbey, who had a grange in Malham.

Across Hanlith Moor

This is a stimulating walk, with a long slow climb to over 1,300 feet (396m). It offers stunning views of the area around Malham, away from the crowds which flock to Malham Cove. A summer walk, when the views are best enjoyed under clear blue skies.

Time: 2½ hours. Distance: 5 miles (8km).
Location: Malham.
Start: Park in Malham National Park Centre car park in the village. (OS grid ref: SD900627.)
OS Map: Outdoor Leisure 2
(Yorkshire Dales – Southern & Western areas)
1:25,000.
See Key to Walks on page 121.

ROUTE DIRECTIONS

From the car park turn left into **Malham**, cross the road and head towards the first small building on the right. Just before the building cross the bridge over the stream and turn right along the path by the river. Go through a gate and through two kissing gates to a signpost directing you left to the waterfall, Janet's Foss. Turn left and follow the path on an easy walk through woodland by the river to **Janet's Foss**. Continue up to the left past the waterfall to reach the road. Turn right on to the road then turn left on to the path signed '**Gordale Scar**'. Follow the path up to the Scar then retrace your steps to return to the road, turn left and continue on up the road.

When you are almost at the top of the hill, turn right on to the track between two walls signed 'Calton'. This leads to the viewpoint known as Weets Cross, beyond which, through the gate and to the left, is the triangulation point for Weets Top at 1,357 feet (414m). From the gate go straight ahead, following the signpost for Calton again, walking parallel to the wall on your right for a few hundred yards until gradually the wall and path converge. Here there is another signpost; follow the path signed 'Hanlith' and cross a stile. The path descends over Hanlith Moor and is clearly marked by yellow marker posts. At the far end of the moor go through the gate on to another walled track which leads down towards **Hanlith** (well worth a visit if you have the time). Before the first house on the right, turn right and pass through a gate on to a footpath signed 'The Pennine Way'. Take this path back towards Malham.

The route here is indicated by yellow markers, which direct you across the pastures, with a wall on your right. At the end of the wall a sign directs you to the right,

Gordale Scar, a high limestone gorge, lies to the east of Malham

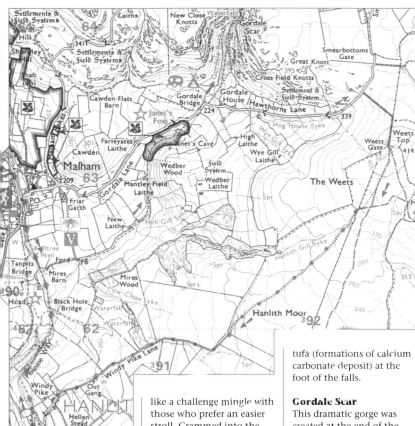

towards a stile next to a gate. Go over the stile, walk parallel to the wall (then fence) on your left and follow the path above the river. After crossing a stream and a stile the path descends towards a gap in the wall and across another bridge to a small stile. Cross another field to the signpost which directed you to Janet's Foss. Continue to Malham and the car park.

POINTS OF INTEREST

Malham
The busiest place in the Dales, where walkers who like a challenge mingle with those who prefer an easier stroll. Crammed into the tiny village are pubs, cafés, places to stay, shops selling camping and walking equipment, and a Yorkshire Dales National Park Centre. The dramatic limestone face of Malham Cove is signposted from the village. Further on are the isolated waters of Malham Tarn (NT and Field Studies Council).

Janet's Foss
Janet, or Jennet, is queen of the local fairies and is reputed to live in a cave behind the falls. Foss is an old Scandinavian word for a waterfall or 'force'. The large pool before the falls has in the past been used by shepherds for dipping their sheep. Note the screen of tufa (formations of calcium carbonate deposit) at the foot of the falls.

Gordale Scar
This dramatic gorge was created at the end of the Carboniferous Period when large shifts in the earth's crust caused this fault and the one at Malham Cove. It is possible to climb up and along the top of the Scar, in between the cliffs and by the stream, but take care in wet weather.

Hanlith
Hanlith, a tiny community which has been here since Anglo-Saxon times, clings to the road that connects it with Kirkby Malham before leading up to Hanlith Moor. Hanlith Hall, originally built in 1668, was altered in the 19th and 20th centuries. Opposite the Hall is a bronze statue of St Francis set into the wall of a house.

DRYSTONE WALLS

Long stretches of drystone walls are a distinctive feature of the landscape of the Dales. Much of the walling dates from the late 1700s and early 1800s; they are easily damaged and hard to repair, so never climb one if there is a gate near by or an alternative route. Walling skills courses are run by the National Trust and the British Trust for Conservation Volunteers.

The arcaded Shambles are set at the heart of the old market town of Settle

SETTLE   North Yorkshire Map ref SD8163

The day to visit Settle is Tuesday – market day – when stalls are crammed into Market Square and visitors must jostle with locals who are in for the day from the surrounding farms and villages. The market charter goes back to 1249. Settle is much smaller than nearby Skipton, but it is a good place for shopping nevertheless, with some old-fashioned family-run stores adding to the appeal of its 18th- and 19th-century buildings.

The composer, Edward Elgar, had a very good friend in Settle, a Dr Buck. Elgar stayed with him often, in his house overlooking the Market Square, where a plaque commemorates the connection. Also overlooking the square is a two-storey row of shops known as the Shambles. In the 17th century this was an open market hall, which later became a butcher's shop. Arches and cottages were added in the 18th century, and then the second storey was built above the cottages in 1898. In front of the Shambles is a fountain pillar erected in 1863 to replace the former market cross, and in front of this is a café with one of the most unusual names you will ever come across: Ye Olde Naked Man Café. It kept the name of an inn, previously on this site, which called itself the Naked Man as a satire on the over-elaborate dressing habits of the time. Ye Olde Naked Woman is in Langcliffe, which is near by. Take a look, if you will, behind Ye Olde Naked Man and you will see Bishopdale Court, typical of the many old yards and alleyways hidden away in Settle's streets.

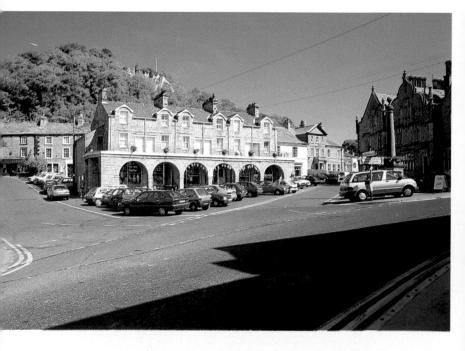

One of the natives of Settle of whom locals are most proud is Benjamin Waugh, who founded the National Society for the Prevention of Cruelty to Children. He was born in a saddler's shop in what is now the Lloyds TSB Bank, off the Market Square. Perhaps Settle's most unusual building is Richard's Folly, on School Hill, not far from the Market Square. The house was built in 1675 for a wealthy local tanner, Richard Preston. He called it Tanner Hall, but it earned its 'folly' nickname because it stood empty for many years, long after Richard's death. It has been restored and a part houses Settle's museum.

West of Settle is its neighbour, Giggleswick, renowned for its public school founded in 1553, and a much quieter place for the visitor to wander. The broadcaster and author Russell Harty lived in Giggleswick. He was once a teacher at Giggleswick School, where he would sometimes take new students out on a hunt for the fabled local treacle mines. Pupils soon lost their scepticism as the trips were often successful, showing that a good practical joke takes a little pre-planning.

To the west of Giggleswick, on the main A65, is the Yorkshire Dales Falconry and Conservation Centre, with a large collection of birds of prey from around the world, many of which are flown and fed during the demonstrations and talks that take place several times a day. There is a lecture theatre as well as a tea room and a well-stocked shop. The outdoor aviaries are built from local limestone which gives a very natural look to the Centre, which is fully committed to both conservation and education.

Enjoy a risqué cream tea at Ye Olde Naked Man Café

FIRST SETTLERS
The first settlers in the Dales are known to have lived, appropriately enough, near Settle. Remains dating back some 10,000 years have been found in the Victoria Cave, about 2 miles (3.2km) north of the town, near Langcliffe. These included bones, flints and other artefacts.

Major Peaks and Minor Dales

This 70-mile (112.7-km) drive takes you through some of the minor but most beautiful dales such as Ribblesdale, Dentdale, Mallerstang, Deepdale and Kingsdale, and passes on the way the Three Peaks: Whernside, Ingleborough and Pen-y-ghent. You will also see the marginally smaller but equally dramatic hills of Wild Boar Fell and High Seat, on the northern boundary of the National Park.

ROUTE DIRECTIONS

See Key to Car Tours on page 120.

The drive starts in Settle which has a helpful Tourist Information Centre and an enterprising museum, as well as busy pubs, cafés and the unusual buildings known as the Shambles. From Settle take the B6480 north to its junction with the A65. Turn right on to the A65 travelling towards Kirkby Lonsdale. Turn right on to the B6255 to Ingleton, put on the map by its unique Waterfalls Walk. It is a small but friendly place with some steep streets, tourist shops and a fine parish church. Follow the signs for 'Village Centre' and then the 'Waterfalls Walk'.

At the start of the Waterfalls Walk, which is marked by a large sign, the road swings sharply left and then right again. Watch for the right turn along here signposted 'Dent'. Follow this road through Thornton in Lonsdale and turn sharp right by the church, still following signs for Dent. This is a narrow, but glorious road through Kingsdale, following Kingsdale Beck, then climbing, with Whernside (2,415 feet/736m) on your right before descending steeply into Deepdale. Turn left at the next junction towards Dent. Continue left through the cobbled streets of Dent, which are delightful but not designed for drivers looking in vain for signposts, until you emerge on the other side.

Continue towards Sedbergh, passing through the very green Dentdale and following the road round to the right. Bear left over the bridge at Millthrop and follow the road signed 'Town Centre'. Go straight on at the roundabout and turn right on to the main street in front of the Reading Room. Sedburgh has a Wednesday market and

A patchwork of fields in pastoral Dentdale on the Cumbrian border

there is also a large livestock market. At the far end turn left, following the signs for Hawes, Kirkby Stephen and Brough.

Follow the A683 alongside the River Rawthey and out of the National Park with dramatic Cautley Spout and the Howgill Fells to your left. From the moors the road descends towards Kirkby Stephen. Turn right on to the A685 into this unspoilt town hidden between the Dales and the Lake District. One attraction is its parish church of St Stephen, with 18th-century bread shelves and a 10th-century Norse stone cross.

In Kirkby Stephen turn right on to the B6259 for Nateby, staying on the road through Nateby and down through the dramatic valley of Mallerstang, with Mallerstang Edge and High Seat (2,329 feet/710m) on your left and Wild Boar Fell on your right. Wild Boar Fell rises to 2,323 feet/708m (higher than Pen-y-ghent at 2,274 feet/693m), and gets its name from the fact that the last wild boar in England was said to have been killed here. Its grandeur and ruggedness remain an imposing sight.

At the T-junction by the Moorcock Inn, turn left on to the A684 towards Hawes, but before you reach the centre of Hawes; turn right on to the B6255 towards Horton in Ribblesdale and Ingleton. This winding road passes through Widdale and up across Gayle Moor, bringing into view on your right the impressive sight of the **Ribblehead Viaduct**, carrying the Settle–Carlisle railway. The railway was built in the late 19th century, and is one of the most impressive feats of Victorian railway engineering. It is the most beautiful route in England,

driving both under and over the Dales. Overlooking the railway is Whernside, the largest of the Three Peaks, closely followed by Ingleborough and finally Pen-y-ghent. Though the smallest of the peaks, the brooding face of Pen-y-ghent has a special appeal.

Just before reaching the viaduct, turn left on to the B6479 passing through Horton in Ribblesdale, Stainforth and on to Settle. This road runs through Ribblesdale with Ingleborough on your right and then the unmistakable looming shape of Pen-y-ghent on your left. The road then runs along the banks of the River Ribble and back down into Settle.

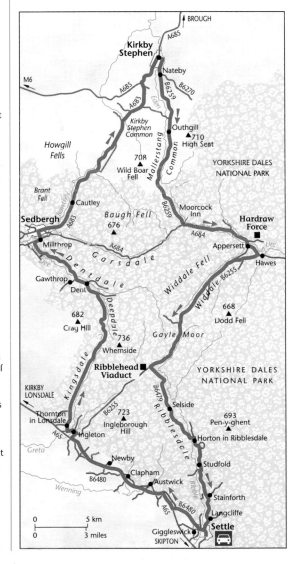

THE YORKSHIRE DALES CYCLE WAY
This almost circular route of 130 miles (209.2km) was devised by John Keavey of the Cyclists' Touring Club, at the request of the National Park Authority, with a view to giving cyclists an enjoyable and safe way of seeing the best that the Dales has to offer. The route begins and ends in Skipton, and is mostly on back roads that are waymarked with blue signs that carry a white cycle and a large direction arrow.
(Continued on next page.)

Skipton Castle, originally the fortress of Robert de Romille, has been altered greatly over the centuries

SKIPTON North Yorkshire Map ref SD9851

Skipton buzzes with life, a busy market fills its main street on four days a week. It has modern shops, ancient inns, churches, a museum, restaurants and hotels, as well as a Norman Castle which is over 900 years old but in a wonderful state of preservation – just like the town itself, in fact. The name of Skipton derives from two Anglo-Saxon words. 'Scipe' means a sheep, while the suffix 'ton' refers to a settlement. You can still find a Sheep Street in Skipton today.

Skipton Castle is one of the most complete and well-preserved medieval castles in England. It was the birthplace of Lady Anne Clifford and bears the Clifford family motto of *Desormais* (Henceforth) in large lettering above the splendid main entrance gate. The castle's importance and huge appeal to visitors is indicated by the fact that there are tour sheets in several languages. Take one to find your own way round its warren of rooms. Some of the original Norman building remains, but most is from the 13th century, later damaged during the Civil War but renovated by Lady Anne Clifford in the mid-17th century.

Beside the castle is Holy Trinity Church, which dates mainly from the 14th and 15th centuries, although a church was on this site as early as the 12th century. It contains the tombs of many of the Clifford family (though not Lady Anne), and a fine Tudor roof and screen are not the least of its attractions.

Castle and church stand at the top of the High Street; half-way down is the Craven Museum, housed in Skipton's Town Hall. There is a small display relating to one of Skipton's most famous sons, Thomas Spencer, of Marks and Spencer, who co-founded the company; other more conventional exhibits depict life ancient and modern in Skipton and the surrounding Craven area. One of the exhibits is a simple piece of cloth that was discovered in one of the Bronze-Age graves near by. It is believed to be the oldest piece of cloth yet discovered in Britain. The museum provides an educational browse, wet or fine.

The oldest building in Skipton's distinguished High Street is the Red Lion Inn. Its exact dates are not known, but it was built in either the late 14th or early 15th centuries and was once partly a farm. The Black Horse Inn is said to have been once owned by Richard III, and yet another coaching inn, the Bay Horse Inn, once stood on the site of what is now the Yorkshire Bank. Still visible in the forecourt is a bear-baiting stone.

But Skipton, like Settle, is a place whose back streets need to be explored, and there are also some very pleasant walks along the canal-side towpaths. Here the Leeds and Liverpool Canal passes through the town, joining on its way the Ellerbeck and Springs Canal, adding to the feel that Skipton, for centuries, really has been the 'Gateway to the Dales'.

Victorian ironwork adorns Skipton's airy Craven Court shopping centre

(Continued from previous page.)

It is suggested that the average cyclist could tackle the route in six days, each day's stage being between 18 and 25 miles (28.9 and 40.2km). There are, inevitably, a few steep sections, with gradients up to 1-in-4 (25%), so be prepared to get off and push, and make sure your brakes are in order when going downhill!

The suggested overnight stops are at Malham, Ingleton, Hawes, Grinton, Kettlewell and Skipton. A folder containing full details and laminated maps for each section is available from National Park Centres and other outlets.

Gateway to The Dales

Leisure Information
Places of Interest
Shopping
Sports, Activities
and the Outdoors
Annual Events and Customs

Checklist

Leisure Information

TOURIST INFORMATION CENTRES

Settle
Town Hall, Cheapside.
Tel: 01729 825192.
Skipton
38 Coach Street. Tel: 01756
792809.

NATIONAL PARK CENTRE

Malham. Tel: 01729 830363.
(There is a 24-hour information
screen.)

OTHER INFORMATION

**British Waterways Board
Headquarters**
Willow Grange, Church Road,
Watford. Tel: 01923 226422.
www.british-waterways.org
English Heritage
37 Tanner Row, York. Tel: 01904
601901.
www.english-heritage.org.uk
Environment Agency
21 Park Square South, Leeds.
Tel: 0113 244 0191.
www.environment-
agency.gov.uk
National Trust
Yorkshire Regional Office
Goddards, 27 Tadcaster Road,
Dringhouses, York.
Tel: 01904 702021.
www.nationaltrust.org.uk

Parking
Visitors are encouraged to use
the pay-and-display car parks at
the National Park Centres to
help relieve traffic congestion in
the villages. Malham, in
particular, gets very busy during
peak holiday periods and at
weekends.
**Yorkshire Dales National
Park Authority**
www.yorkshiredales.org.uk
Yorkshire Museums Council
www.yorkshiremuseums.org.uk
Yorkshire Tourist Board
www.ytb.org.uk
Yorkshire Wildlife Trust
10 Toft Green, York.
Tel: 01904 659570.
www.yorkshire-wildlife-
trust.org.uk

ORDNANCE SURVEY MAPS

Landranger 1:50,000 Sheets 98,
103, 104.
Outdoor Leisure 1:25,000 Sheet
10.

Places of Interest

There will be an admission
charge at the following places of
interest unless otherwise stated.
Bentham Pottery
Bentham.
Tel: 01524 261567. Open all
year, Mon–Sat.

Bolton Abbey Estate
Bolton Abbey. Priory ruins
beside river. Tel: 01756
718009. Open all year, Apr–Oct
daily; Nov–Mar weekends only.
Fee for the car park.
Broughton Hall
Skipton. Tel: 01756 792267.
Open Apr–Sep for organised
tours only. Write to the Estate
Office, Broughton Hall, Skipton,
BD23 3AE.
Craven Museum
First Floor, Town Hall, High
Street, Skipton. Tel: 01756
706407. Large collection on
Craven life, from prehistoric
times to the present day. Open
Apr–Sep, closed Tue; Oct–Mar
closed Tue & Sun.
**Embsay and Bolton Abbey
Steam Railway**
Skipton. Tel: 01756 710614
(general) or 01756 795189
(talking timetable). Rides to
Dales villages for walks and
picnic spots. Collection of
engines and well-stocked shop
at Embsay. Open Sun all year;
additional days Apr–Sep.
Telephone to check.
Linton Court Gallery
Duke Street, Settle. Regular
exhibitions. Tel: 01729 822695.
Not open on a regular basis.
Telephone to check.

Skipton Castle
Tel: 01756 792442. Very well-preserved 12th-century castle complete with dungeon. Open all year daily, except 25 Dec.

Yorkshire Dales Falconry and Conservation Centre
On the A65 near Giggleswick. Tel: 01729 825164. Owls, hawks, falcons and eagles are among the birds to be seen here. Flying displays daily. Open all year most days, daily in summer.

Yorkshire Dales National Park Centre
Malham. Tel: 01729 830363. The centre stocks a wide range of literature about the area, there are displays on the natural history, the local community and the work of conservation bodies. 24-hour information screen. Open Apr–Oct daily, limited winter opening. Free.

SPECIAL INTEREST FOR CHILDREN

The following places may be of interest to visitors with children. Unless otherwise stated there will be an admission charge.

Bentham Pottery
Bentham. Tel: 01524 261567. Visitors can watch demonstrations of throwing, firing and decorating. Pottery for sale. Open all year Mon–Sat.

Bolton Abbey Estate
Bolton Abbey. Tel: 01756 718009.Priory ruins beside river, 30 miles (48km) of walks around the estate, including the Strid Wood Nature Trails. Open all year daily Apr–Oct; weekends only Nov–Mar. Fee for car park.

Embsay and Bolton Abbey Steam Railway
Skipton. Tel: 01756 710614 (general) or 01756 795189 (talking timetable). Rides to Dales villages for walks and picnic spots. Collection of engines and well-stocked shop at Embsay. Open Sun all year; additional days Apr–Sep. Telephone to check.

Skipton Castle
Tel: 01756 792442. Very well-preserved 12th-century castle with dungeon. Open all year daily, except Christmas Day.

Watershed Mill Craft Centre
Watershed Mill, Langcliffe Road, Settle. Tel: 01729 85111. Craft showrooms, fossil shop, children's art activity centre. Open all year, daily except Christmas Day and Easter Sunday.

Yorkshire Dales Falconry and Conservation Centre
On the A65 near Giggleswick. Tel: 01729 825164. Owls, hawks, falcons and eagles are among the birds to be seen here. Flying displays daily. Open all year most days.

Shopping

Settle
Open-air market Tue.

Skipton
Craven Court is a covered shopping centre in restored buildings. Open-air market Mon, Wed, Fri and Sat.

Embsay Steam and Bolton Abbey Railway offers short but scenic rides

LOCAL SPECIALITIES

Crafts
Watershed Mill Craft Centre, Watershed Mill, Langcliffe Road, Settle. Tel: 01729 825111. Craft showroom, children's art activity centre. Open all year, daily except Christmas Day and Easter Sunday.
Dorothy Ward, The Barn, Gargrave. Lamps, pottery, baskets, woollen goods. Tel: 01756 749275.

Local Books and Maps
Archway Books, Commercial Court, Settle. Tel: 01729 824009.

Outdoor Equipment
Cave and Crag, Market Place, Settle. Tel: 01729 823877.
Cove Centre, Wallbridge Mill, Cove Road, Malham. Tel: 01729 830432.
George Fisher, 1 Coach Street, Skipton. Tel: 01756 794305.

Paintings and Photographs of the Dales
Dales Pictures, Church Street, Settle. Tel: 01729 823123.

Pottery
Bentham Pottery, Bentham. Tel: 01524 261567. Visitors can watch demonstrations; details of courses on application. Items made at the pottery, including ceramic murals are for sale.

Walking Sticks
Many 'outdoor' shops sell traditional Dales carved walking sticks, which are normally hand-carved from pieces of ash, blackthorn, hazel or holly.

Sports, Activities and the Outdoors

ANGLING

Fly
Coniston Cold A 24-acre lake on Coniston Hall Estate. Tel: 01756 749551 or through the hotel on 01756 748080. Open daily.
Skipton Fishing on the River Aire in and around Skipton. Permits are available from the post office in Embsay. Tel: 01756 793308.

BALLOON FLIGHTS

Skipton
Airborne Adventures, Old Burton Croft, Rylstone. Tel: 01756 730166.

BOAT HIRE

Skipton
For information about boat hire contact Skipton Tourist Information Centre. Tel: 01756 792809.

BOAT TRIPS

Skipton
Various companies operate boat trips along the Leeds and Liverpool Canal including Pennine Boat Trips of Skipton, Waterside Court, Coach Street. Tel: 01756 790829. Details of other operaters from Skipton Tourist Information Centre. Tel: 01756 792809.

CLIMBING

Bolton Abbey
Facilities available at Eastby Crag. Permission must be obtained from the Chatsworth Estate at Bolton Abbey. Tel: 01756 710227.

CYCLING

The Yorkshire Dales Cycle Way
A 130-mile (209.2-km) circular route that starts and ends in Skipton.

CYCLE HIRE

Skipton
Dave Ferguson Cycles, 1 Brook Street. Tel: 01756 795367. Also at Bowbridge Garage, Skipton Road, Embsay. Tel: 01756 792526.

GOLF COURSES

Settle
Settle Golf Club, Buckhaw Brow, Giggleswick. Tel: 01729 825288.

Skipton
Skipton Golf Club, off north-western bypass. Tel: 01756 795657/793922.

GOLF DRIVING RANGE

White Hills Golf Driving Range, Stirton, Skipton. Tel: 01756 793325.

GUIDED WALKING HOLIDAYS

Week long or short break holidays walking in the Dales are organised by: HF Holidays Ltd,

Imperial House, Edgware Road, London. Tel: 020 8905 9558.

HORSE-RIDING

Conistone
Kilnsey Trekking and Riding Centre, Homestead Farm. Tel: 01756 752861. Lessons, trekking, trail rides and weekly holidays available.

LONG-DISTANCE FOOTPATHS AND TRAILS

The Cavendish 27 Circuit
A 27-mile (43.4-km) walk through the southern half of the Yorkshire Dales National Park starting at Bolton Abbey.

The Six Dales Hike
A 42-mile (67.6-km) walk through North Yorkshire from Settle to Skipton.

Annual Events and Customs

Malham
Malham Show, late August.

Settle
Maypole celebrations at Long Preston, May Day.

Skipton
Skipton Gala, early June.
Game Fair, held at Broughton Hall, late June.

The checklists give details of just some of the facilities within the area covered by this guide. Further information can be obtained from Tourist Information Centres.

Relax awhile in Skipton, 'Gateway to the Dales'

Harrogate and Ripon

This is the 'civilised' corner of the Dales, where the landscape is pleasantly rolling – even flat in places – and will appeal particularly to car drivers and those who like strolling round sights, rather than serious walkers who prefer to trek across the high hills of the wilder Dales. It contains one of Britain's most visited and most scenic attractions in Fountains Abbey, magnificent even in its ruined state, surrounded by the

beautifully landscaped Studley Royal Gardens. There is the cathedral city of Ripon to explore, refined Harrogate, with its colourful parks and gardens, and the stately splendours of Newby Hall... not to mention Old Mother Shipton's Cave in Knaresborough.

BRIMHAM ROCKS North Yorkshire Map ref SE2165
Found just off the B6265, 4 miles (6.4km) east of Pateley Bridge, these 50 acres (20ha) of rocks standing in the Nidderdale moorland should not be missed. Nowhere will you see a sight quite like them – blocks and boulders of 20 feet (6m) and more in height, weathered simply by wind, rain, frost and ice into strange and surreal shapes. They have been a tourist attraction since the 18th century, and over the years some have inevitably acquired names, such as the Blacksmith and Anvil, the Sphinx, the Indian Turban and the Dancing Bear, giving some idea of the shapes these rocks of dark millstone grit have been twisted into. So strange are these shapes that it is hard to believe they were not created by a team of sculptors, or even by some playful god. One in particular, known as the Idol, is huge and seems to be improbably balanced on a rock scarcely the size of a dinner plate. There is also a Kissing Chair and the inevitable Lover's Leap.

There is a car park at the entrance of the site, and a choice of several walks through the area, which in all extends for 387 acres (157ha) around the rocks themselves. Some paths go off into the undergrowth, but an easier central path leads to Brimham House, converted into an information centre with refreshment facilities and a shop attached. A viewing platform indicates the sights for some distance all around.

BRIMHAM MOOR
The area of the rocks and surrounding moorland appears in the Domesday Book as Birnbeam, and at that time the land was, like much of the Dales, forested. The monks of Fountains Abbey cleared the trees from the landscape to enable them to farm it, thus also exposing the rocks to the elements, although the basic shapes were created about a million years ago during the Ice Age, the ice working on rocks that were first deposited some 200 million years ago.

The exquisite ruins of Fountains Abbey

ROLL OUT THE EGGS

Parents of young children might like to know that the Easter Monday egg-rolling tradition was revived at Fountains Abbey in the 1980s, at the suggestion of an estate worker who recalled it from his own childhood. Hard-boiled eggs are thrown or rolled down a hill, a prize being given to the one which goes the furthest before disintegrating completely. In some places in Yorkshire, children would decorate their eggs first and put them on display, before rolling them down the nearest slope and finally eating any that remained edible.

FOUNTAINS ABBEY North Yorkshire Map ref SE2768

To describe Fountains Abbey as a ruin does it a disservice, and even the term 'remains' does not prepare the visitor for the awesome and graceful sight of the best-preserved Cistercian abbey in Britain. It looks as if it may have been only a few years ago that the monks finally moved out. Fountains Abbey was justifiably designated a World Heritage Site in 1987, and is one of the largest monastic ruins in Europe.

Fountains Abbey was first founded in 1132 by monks who left a Benedictine abbey in York because the order was not strict enough for them. The buildings you see today were mostly constructed in the years from 1150 to 1250, though the North Tower that looms up into the sky is a 16th-century addition. This is called Huby's Tower, named for Marmaduke Huby, the abbot who had it built not long before the Dissolution of the Monasteries.

In medieval times Fountains Abbey was the richest abbey in Britain; it owned a great deal of the land in the Yorkshire Dales, and used it for grazing large herds of cattle and sheep. Visitors travelling around the Dales today will come across constant references to land that once belonged to the abbey, and buildings that were once its granges (outlying farms). Sheep-rearing and the resultant meat and cheese produced was a large source of revenue for the monks, and visitors can only try to imagine the wealth that would ensue if one estate owned and farmed the same area of land today.

A visitor centre was added in 1992 amid some controversy and fears that it would intrude on the beauty of the abbey itself, but hidden away as it is, the centre caters well for the 300,000 people who visit the site each year. Its design ensures that while Huby's Tower can be seen from the centre, to give a sense of the abbey's presence, the modern centre cannot be seen while wandering round the abbey. The visitor centre incorporates an auditorium, a restaurant and the largest National Trust shop in Britain.

The adjoining grounds of Studley Royal were created in the early 18th century and then merged with Fountains Abbey in 1768. They were the life's work of John Aislabie, and subsequently his son, William. John Aislabie inherited the estate in 1699 when he was Treasurer of the Navy. He later became Chancellor of the Exchequer, but involvement in the disastrous South Sea Bubble left him free to spend more time with his garden. The landscaping took 14 years, then another decade for the construction of the buildings. There are several paths around the gardens, through which the River Skell flows, and a map is recommended as there is a great deal to see including temples and cascades. Nineteenth-century St Mary's Church, built by William Burges, is the focal point of the 400-acre (162ha) deer park, home to herds of about 350 red, fallow and Manchurian sika deer.

THE SOUTH SEA BUBBLE

The South Sea Company, formed in 1711, monopolised trade in the South Seas and South America. The bubble 'burst' in 1720, and in the following year John Aislabie, Chancellor of the Exchequer, was sent to the Tower of London charged with fraud. He served a short sentence and was then dispatched back to the north of England, his career in ruins. He appears to have had some money left over, judging by the extent of the work done on Studley Royal, for which 100 men would be employed each year for the manual work alone.

A perfect symmetry of arches in the cellarium

THE AGATHA CHRISTIE MYSTERY

The famous crime writer, inventor of Miss Marple and other detectives, was herself involved in a mystery in 1926 when she went missing. She had discovered that her husband was having an affair, and disappeared for several days. After a great deal of speculation in the newspapers, she was eventually found in the Swan Hotel in Harrogate, where she was staying under a false name. Why she chose the Swan Hotel, and Harrogate, and whether she had lost her memory or not, remain a mystery. The story was turned into a film starring Dustin Hoffman and Vanessa Redgrave, and filmed on location in the town where it happened.

Harrogate is a delightful gateway to the Dales – don't miss the famous Betty's tea rooms

HARROGATE North Yorkshire Map ref SE3054

Although not within the Yorkshire Dales as such, Harrogate is by far the largest town on their fringes, and a magnet for anyone with serious shopping – or window-shopping – to be done. It is an attractive and lively place with theatres, cinemas and good restaurants, and a plethora of hotels and modern conference centres created by the conference industry. But Harrogate has not lost its charm, and the spa town that first developed after the discovery of a spring in 1571 is still plainly visible.

A most important feature of Harrogate is its greenery, especially the wide swathes of grass and flower beds known as the Stray that sweeps right through the town. These 200 acres (81ha) are protected under an ancient law which ensures that residents and visitors alike are entitled to enjoy these recreational facilities. There are more flowers as well as a boating pond, children's playground, crazy golf and other activities in the Valley Gardens, Harrogate's main park. Its entrance is close to the Royal Pump Room Museum.

Flower lovers will not want to miss a visit to the Harlow Carr Botanical Gardens on the outskirts of Harrogate off the B6162. This is the headquarters of the Northern Horticultural Society, set in 68 impressive acres (28ha), a lovely mix of the formal and informal, with a gardening museum, plant and gift shops, and refreshments. Courses, demonstrations and practical workshops are held in the Study Centre.

Harrogate's origins can be traced in the octagonal Royal Pump Room Museum, which was built in 1842 in order to enclose the old sulphur well on this site. In

addition to serving up local history the museum still serves up cups of the pungent spa water that made the town famous. It claims to be the strongest sulphur water in Europe, so some visitors may prefer Perrier, or to refresh the palate with a visit afterwards to Betty's tea rooms, a Yorkshire institution offering delicious cream cakes and Yorkshire Fat Rascals.

Not quite a Yorkshire institution is a visit to a Turkish baths, and perhaps it is just a coincidence that the entrance to the baths is a short stroll down Cambridge Road from Betty's. Harrogate is one of the few places where you can enjoy a Turkish bath in its original 19th-century splendour at the Harrogate Turkish and Sauna Suite in the Royal Baths Assembly Rooms. Its Victorian exterior masks a beautifully renovated tiled interior, with a cold plunge bath, several hot rooms, a steam room, massage room and a relaxing rest room for when the ordeal is over. There are both male and female sessions, so check first if you are thinking of going along.

The Harrogate Volunteer Guided Walks Group consists of local people with a special interest in the history of Harrogate, and they conduct guided tours of the town, with two options. Low Harrogate tours last one hour and begin outside the Royal Pump Room Museum, while tours of High Harrogate start at the main entrance to Christ Church on the Stray and last for approximately 90 minutes. Details of the dates and times of these free and fascinating tours are available from the Tourist Information Centre.

A brilliant show of spring flowers in Harrogate's Valley Gardens

THE ENGLISH SPA

It was because of a spring discovered here that the word spa entered the English language. William Slingsby of nearby Bilton Hall had visited the town of Spa, then in Germany, which was noted for its health-giving waters. While out riding or walking in 1571 near the tiny village of Haregate, outside Knaresborough, he came across a freshwater spring, attracted to it by the numbers of lapwings near by. When he drank the water it reminded him of the waters at Spa, and he walled off the spring and called it the Tewit Well – tewit is a northern name for the lapwing. When other medicinal springs were discovered near by, Haregate became a spa town, known now as Harrogate.

THE HOUSE IN THE ROCK

This folly was carved out of the rock face by a local weaver, and is still lived in as a private dwelling. It can be found up the steps by St Robert's Chapel, also carved out of the rock in 1408. The Chapel is off Abbey Road, beyond Low Bridge.

Knaresborough's Castle, once a significant stronghold, was reduced to a dramatic shell by Parliamentary forces after the Civil War

KNARESBOROUGH   North Yorkshire Map ref SE3557

Knaresborough is one of the most picturesque market towns in the Dales, much of it perched on ridges of rock that rise above the River Nidd, on which rowing boats are usually bobbing about. A viaduct crosses high above the river, while old houses peek through the trees on one side, looking across at the parkland and woods which conceal Mother Shipton's Cave on the opposite bank.

In the time of the Yorkshire prophetess, Mother Shipton, much of this land was a large hunting forest, and Knaresborough must have looked even more beautiful than it does now. Mother Shipton is said to have been born in the cave in 1488 during a violent storm, and she later gained a reputation for the accuracy of her prophecies. It is claimed that she foretold the attempted invasion and eventual defeat of the Spanish Armada in 1588, and predicted the Great Fire of London in 1666. The cave can be visited as part of a guided tour, along with the Petrifying Well – in which minerals in the water turn any object placed inside it to stone – and a small museum.

The town's official museum is up in the Old Courthouse in the grounds of Knaresborough Castle. It houses a small collection of local items and a gallery devoted to the Civil War in Knaresborough, but is enjoyable not least because Knaresborough seems to have had more than its fair share of characters over the years, and their doings are well chronicled. In addition to Mother Shipton there was Robert Flower, who lived in a cave by the river and was known as St Robert because of his alleged miraculous healing powers; Eugene Aram,

a schoolmaster who murdered a shoemaker in St Robert's cave and escaped justice for 13 years; and John Metcalfe, who went blind at the age of six, but later went on to become a quantity surveyor, road building pioneer, accomplished violinist and part-time smuggler!

Little remains of Knaresborough Castle, but it has also seen its fair share of characters over the years. The murderers of Thomas à Becket sought refuge here for a time, and royal visitors included Edward III, King John and Richard II, who was imprisoned here in 1399. The dungeon remains just as it was. There are guides on hand to answer questions, and regular tours of the sallyport (a secret access to the moat). With a small park around the remains, this is a popular spot with locals, who come to sit and enjoy the lovely views over the river.

Not far away is the market place, where as well as a very busy Wednesday market you will find the oldest chemist's shop in the country, believed to have been first established on the site as long ago as the 13th century, but continuously trading since 1720. The market is first mentioned in 1206, but is known to have been held each and every Wednesday since 1310, the day fixed by Edward II's charter.

The Church of St John contains some Norman remains, and a Tudor font with a lockable cover to prevent witches stealing the holy water. By the church, a street named Water Bag Bank descends steeply to the river. The unusual name arose because the town's water supply was once brought up here on horseback in leather bags.

The River Nidd flows through Knaresborough

GUIDED WALKS

A free introduction to Knaresborough is available by taking one of the guided walks conducted by local volunteers who have a good knowledge of the thousands of years of history behind their town. This scheme was set up in 1994, after the success of a similar scheme in neighbouring Harrogate. Guides introduce you to the many characters who have lived in or visited Knaresborough, from Mother Shipton to Oliver Cromwell. The hour-long tours take place several times a week from late May to late September, with further details available from the Tourist Information Centre.

THE NEWGATE CONNECTION

As you approach the Garden Restaurant, an old wooden door on the left of the entrance gates bears an intriguing inscription: 'Through these gates Jack Sheppard, highwayman, escaped from Newgate Prison, 30th August 1724'. The Lord Mayor of London at that time was an ancestor of the Vyner family, who came to Newby Hall in the mid-19th century.

The charming 18th-century mansion of Newby Hall was designed by Robert Adam and incorporates an elaborate tapestry room and two galleries of Roman sculpture

NEWBY HALL North Yorkshire Map ref SE3468

Newby Hall is rather hidden away in the countryside southeast of Ripon, but it is well worth seeking out even though it is inevitably busy on summer weekends and Bank Holidays. The 18th-century mansion, designed by Robert Adam and one of the finest stately homes in this part of the world, is signposted off the B6265 Ripon–Boroughbridge road, near the village of Skelton.

Although there are no guided tours, staff are on hand in the rooms and corridors to answer any questions you might have. An informative booklet gives details of the many rooms that are on public view. The billiard room is particularly splendid, and contains a portrait of Frederick Grantham Vyner, an ancestor who was murdered by Greek bandits. There is a fine statue gallery, a great deal of Chippendale furniture to admire, an overwhelming tapestry room, its walls covered in 18th-century French tapestries, and, by way of contrast, an amusing collection in the chamber pot room.

Outside the hall, the award-winning gardens are extensive and will appeal as much to horticultural experts for their contents as to those who can simply admire the beauty of their design. The credit for their development goes to the present owner's father, Major Edward Compton, who transformed the grounds from a 9-hole golf course into gardens of floral splendour that have been specifically created to offer something

different in every season of the year. More than that, Newby Hall offers visitors a choice of leaflets suggesting the best walks to appreciate the seasonal highlights. Many other leaflets are available, for the general visitor who might want to take the Woodland Discovery Walk (a delightful nature trail) or the specialist interested in the National Collection of *Cornus* (Dogwood), which is held here.

The Woodland Discovery Walk is a particularly attractive stroll through an orchard, down to the River Ure, crossing a restored rustic bridge and back up to Newby Hall through Bragget Wood. In the woods watch out for tree creepers and nuthatches, and down by the river for the flash of blue that indicates a kingfisher. Mammals are less evident, and no doubt the owners wish one of them was even less evident, given the damage caused by grey squirrels. But the more peaceful water vole might be seen in the river, and in summer butterflies and bees fill the air. For plant lovers there are foxgloves and ferns, snowdrops and bluebells in season, and more unusual items such as Indian Balsam and Persian Ivy. The walk has been created with the help of the Yorkshire Wildlife Trust, hence the wealth of information in the available booklet.

Children have not been neglected at Newby Hall, as there is a miniature railway, complete with engine shed and signal box, which runs along the banks of the River Ure, and near by are an adventure playground, a paddling pool, paddle boats and a duck pond. There is a large picnic area, a licensed restaurant, a plant stall, and a very well-stocked shop and information centre. A variety of special events are held throughout the year.

Ferns and fuchsias flourish in a shady corner of the garden at Newby Hall

MURDERED AT MARATHON

In 1870 Frederick Grantham Vyner, brother-in-law of the Earl of Ripon, joined a group of distinguished British tourists in Greece. After visiting the site of the Battle of Marathon, the group set out to return to their base in Athens, a marathon's distance away. En route they were captured by bandits, who set a high ransom for their release as the group included several members of the British aristocracy. The ransom was agreed, but the soldiers delivering it opened fire on the bandits, who murdered their captives. Frederick Grantham Vyner's mother used her share of the rescued ransom money to build a church in memory of her son, and this is the Church of Christ the Consoler at Skelton-cum-Newby, in the grounds of the Newby Hall estate.

AN UNCULTIVATED PLACE
'At Pateley Bridge the vicar
afforded me the use of his
church. Though it was more
than twice as large as our
preaching-house, it was not
near large enough to contain
the congregation. How vast is
the increase of the work of God!
Particularly in the most rugged
and uncultivated places! '
From John Wesley's Journal

PATELEY BRIDGE North Yorkshire Map ref SE1565
The main attraction at Pateley Bridge is the Nidderdale
Museum, but the town is also a good base for visiting
places of interest near by. Many of the buildings date
from the 18th and 19th centuries, when the town
flourished with thriving local industries and the arrival
of the railway, though as it is built of dark gritstone it
can seem a dour place in gloomy weather.

There is nothing dour about the award-winning
Nidderdale Museum, housed in the town's council
offices. It was founded in 1975 and grew from a tiny
collection to one which today tells you all you need to
know about life in Nidderdale, from the spread of
religion and the development of transport to collections
of cameras and razors that have all been owned by local
people. Some of the most enjoyable exhibits are the
reconstructed cobbler's shop, general store, milliner's
shop, joiner's shop and solicitor's office. All contain
fascinating memorabilia, and the whole museum is
much loved and well looked after.

To the north of Pateley Bridge, near Lofthouse, is How
Stean Gorge, popularly known as Yorkshire's 'Little
Switzerland'. The ravine of up to 80 feet (24m) deep was
hacked out in the Ice Age. Pathways lead along by the
fast-flowing river through ferns and by lush, dank
undergrowth; there are bridges on different levels and
fenced galleries on rocky ledges. There are also a few
caves, the best known being Tom Taylor's Cave, with a
530-foot (162-m) walk underground (torch needed).

To the west of Pateley Bridge on the B6265 are the
Stump Cross Caverns. Only discovered in the mid-19th
century, the caves have given up fossil bones as much as
200,000 years old, many from the wild animals such as
bison, reindeer and wolverines that once wandered here.
Visitors can also see the usual stalactites and stalagmites
with appropriate names.

*Racing water has carved
How Stean Gorge from solid
rock*

RIPLEY   North Yorkshire Map ref SE2860

Ripley is an estate village built around Ripley Castle, which has been home to the Ingilby family since the 1320s. Hour-long guided tours are available, with the guides providing many colourful anecdotes about the castle's past owners and visitors. A plasterwork ceiling was put into the Tower Room with the specific intention of impressing James VI of Scotland as he passed through on his way to becoming King James I of England. There are fine collections of weaponry and furniture, as well as secret hiding holes and passageways.

The Gardens contain the National Hyacinth Collection, as well as walled gardens, old hothouse buildings and a walk through the wooded grounds to take in a hilltop gazebo. One of the herbaceous borders in the walled gardens is no less than 120 yards (110m) long, making not merely a splash of colour but a positive swimming pool.

Ripley village was largely built in the 1820s by Sir William Amcotts Ingilby, an affable eccentric who modelled it on an estate village he had seen in Alsace-Lorraine. The delightful result is the only place in Yorkshire which has a 'Hotel de Ville' rather than a Town Hall, and the cobbled Market Square with its stocks, the listed cottages with their window boxes, and the 15th-century church all make this an unusual and pleasurable place to visit.

Ripley Castle lies just north of Harrogate

TROOPER JANE

An ancestor of character was undoubtedly Jane Ingilby, who became known as Trooper Jane. She helped her brother, Sir William, raise a troop of horsemen from Ripley and went to the assistance of the Royalist army beseiging York. Disguised as a man and wearing a full suit of armour, this doughty lady not only fought at Marston Moor but also saved her brother's life in defeat by hiding him in a priest hole. Oliver Cromwell arrived at Ripley that night demanding admittance. Jane allowed him to sleep in an armchair in the library, sitting opposite him with a pair of pistols hidden in her lap, to ensure her brother was not discovered.

To Small Towns and Large Villages

Middleham, with its market and castle, is the smallest town in the Yorkshire Dales – much smaller than many villages. This 75-mile (120.7-km) drive takes in some of the attractive places that hover between town and village, such as Kettlewell, Grassington, Leyburn and Pateley Bridge, where the tour starts.

ROUTE DIRECTIONS

See Key to Car Tours on page 120.

The drive starts in Pateley Bridge, a lively market town in the heart of Nidderdale with its own local museum, shopping and Tourist Information Centre. From the centre of Pateley Bridge take the minor road that leads north from near the bridge itself, towards Ramsgill and Lofthouse. Pass Gouthwaite Reservoir on your right. In Lofthouse turn right and take the steep road out of the village, over the moors towards Masham. Continue for about 6 miles (9.7km), passing two more reservoirs on the right. Take the third left turn, as you approach Healey, towards Ellingstring, turning left again to the junction with the A6108. Turn left

at the crossroads and continue to the junction with the A6108. Turn left on to the A6108 to Leyburn passing the impressive remains of **Jervaulx Abbey** on the right. The Abbey, founded in 1156, is in complete contrast to the grand and busy Fountains Abbey, yet in its day it was one of the most important Cistercian abbeys in Yorkshire. Continue on the A6108 and pass through Middleham, considered to be 'the Newmarket of the north', with its 16 or so racing stables. The impressive ruined castle was much favoured by Richard III, whose son Edward was born here in 1473.

Continue to Leyburn, a busy Wensleydale town with many tea shops for visitors as well as a wealth of everyday

shops. In Leyburn turn left then right following signs 'A6108 Richmond'. The road first takes you over upland pasture then along the wooded Alpine-like slopes of the River Swale towards Richmond. At this point you can take a detour and continue into Richmond which stands at the foot of Swaledale, the castle commanding an impressive position above the river. The town has a large cobbled square, a church with shops in its side, riverside walks and three museums, all worth seeing.

If you are not taking the detour, continue as before and as you reach Richmond pass a right turn to Catterick, turn immediately left up Hurgill Road, past a car park on the left. This road takes you back along the Swale but climbs high above the river, before dropping steeply down to Marske.

Cross the bridge and turn right towards Reeth, then turn left on to the B6270 to Grinton. In Grinton turn right on to a minor road and take the right fork following the signs for Redmire. This is an impressive high moorland road passing disused lead mines. When the road finally

The extensive church of St Andrew at Grinton

descends, take the first turning right for Castle Bolton then turn right for Carperby. Take a left turn to **Aysgarth Falls** – a very popular beauty spot. Although they consist of three different sections, only the Upper Falls are visible from the road. Near by are a mill, a carriage museum and tearooms, while Aysgarth village itself is another half-mile (0.8km) away, on the main Wensleydale road.

Beyond Aysgarth Falls turn left on to the A684 signposted Leyburn then take the second turning on the right on to the B6160 following the signs into West Burton, which has been described as the prettiest village in the Dales. It certainly has the largest village green, on which horses graze and children play. In the centre there is a pub and a pottery, but no church or market. A waterfall, Burton Force, is a short stroll away.

Rejoin the B6160 which now takes you along the

lovely and lesser-known Bishopdale, over Kidstones Pass to Buckden in Wharfedale. Pass Kettlewell on the left, a small busy town and a centre for walkers tackling nearby Great Whernside. It is also on the Dales Way long-distance footpath, and was once a centre of the lead-mining industry.

Continue ahead and look out for **Kilnsey Crag** on your right, easily identified as it juts out dramatically towards the

main road. Kilnsey Crag is popular with climbers, film-makers and peregrine falcons. Continue on the B6160 then turn left into the centre of Grassington – an attractive, large village with narrow cobbled streets, 17th- and 18th-century houses, pubs and a museum of Upper Wharfedale life. Drive around the centre of Grassington, leave on the B6265 and return to Nidderdale and Pateley Bridge.

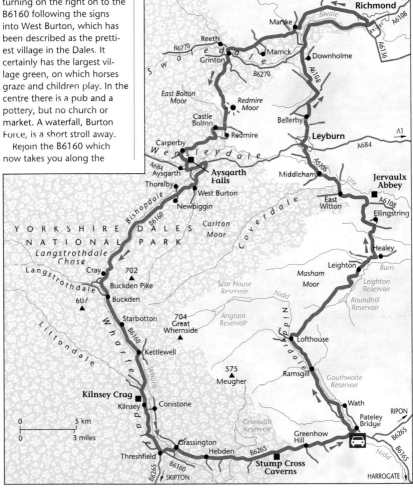

SOUND TRADITIONS

Every night at 9pm the Ripon Hornblower blows his horn in the market place and then once more outside the home of the Mayor. The ceremony marks the setting of the watch, letting the citizens know that their safe-keeping overnight was the responsibility of the wakeman. The office of wakeman disappeared in 1604, but the tradition lives on. Also at 9pm, the curfew bell at Ripon Cathedral is sounded (unless a concert is taking place). This custom comes from the Normans, when it was an instruction that all fires should be covered for the night – a safety precaution in the days of timber houses. The word curfew comes from the French, *couvre-feu* – cover the fire.

Ripon's magnificent cathedral

RIPON   North Yorkshire Map ref SE3171

In AD 672 St Wilfrid built a church on the site of what is now Ripon Cathedral, and the crypt of that church can still be visited, making it the oldest complete Saxon crypt in any English cathedral. The west front of this splendid cathedral dates from 1220, the east front from 1290, and inside there are 500-year-old woodcarvings, a 16th-century nave and some exceptional stained-glass work. All in all, a building not to be missed.

Close by, in St Mary's Gate, visitors move from God to the Godless, in the Ripon Prison and Police Museum. Housed in the cell block of what was first the Ripon Liberty Prison and later its Police Station, the museum tells the vivid story of Yorkshire law and disorder through the ages. It has some chilling but never gruesome displays.

All around Ripon attractions vie for attention. The Lightwater Valley Amusement Park, with its enormous rollercoasters and other rides, is high on the list for families. There are, naturally, lots of eating places and gift shops, and – to appeal, no doubt, to parents while they let their children loose on the rides – there is the Lightwater Village, a shopping centre with factory, fashion and food shops.

Two miles (3.2km) east of Lightwater Valley, but for more refined tastes, is Norton Conyers, a country house which dates back to the mid-14th century. Visitors will hear the legend of the Mad Woman, a story also heard by Charlotte Brontë when she visited the house in 1839. The character in the story was possibly the inspiration for the mad Mrs Rochester in *Jane Eyre* written eight years later, but there are other claimants to this honour.

Harrogate and Ripon

Leisure Information
Places of Interest
Shopping
The Performing Arts
Sports, Activities
and the Outdoors
Annual Events and Customs

Checklist

Leisure Information

TOURIST INFORMATION CENTRES

Harrogate
Royal Baths, Crescent Road. Tel: 01423 537300.
Knaresborough
9 Castle Courtyard. Tel: 01423 866886.
Pateley Bridge
18 High Street. Tel: 01423 711147.
Ripon
Minster Road. Tel: 01765 604625.

OTHER INFORMATION

British Waterways Board Headquarters
Willow Grange, Church Road, Watford. Tel: 01923 226422.
www.british-waterways.org
English Heritage
37 Tanner Row, York. Tel: 01904 601901.
www.english-heritage.org.uk
Environment Agency
21 Park Square South, Leeds.
Tel: 0113 244 0191.
www.environment-agency.gov.uk
National Trust
Yorkshire Regional Office:
Goddards, 27 Tadcaster Road,
Dringhouses, York. Tel: 01904 702021.
www.nationaltrust.org.uk
Parking
Limited free disc parking is available in Harrogate and Knaresborough, usually up to two hours. Discs can normally be obtained from Tourist Information Centres, shops, banks etc. Parking is particularly difficult in the narrow streets at the centre of Knaresborough, however, and visitors would be advised to use one of the pay-and-display car parks.
Yorkshire Wildlife Trust
10 Toft Green, York. Tel: 01904 659570. www.yorkshire-wildlife-trust.org.uk

ORDNANCE SURVEY MAPS

Landranger 1:50,000 Sheets 99, 104.
Explorer 1:25,000 Sheets 26, 27.

Places of Interest

There will be an admission charge at the following places of interest unless otherwise stated.
Brimham Rocks
Southwest of Brimham off the B6265. Tel: 01423 780688.
The spectacular rock formations stand at a height of 950 feet (289.5m) in open moorland, owned by the National Trust. Open access to moors. NT shop open Jun–Sep daily; Apr, May and Oct weekends and Bank Hols.
Fountains Abbey and Studley Royal
Ripon. Tel: 01765 608888.
Open all year, most days.
Harlow Carr Botanical Gardens
Crag Lane, Otley Road, Harrogate.
Tel: 01423 565418.
Ornamental and woodland gardens extending to over 58 acres. Open all year, daily.
Harrogate Turkish Baths and Sauna Suite
Parliament Street, Harrogate.
Tel: 01423 556746 for details.
Open daily.
How Stean Gorge
near Lofthouse, Pateley Bridge.
Tel: 01423 755666. Open all year, most days.
Knaresborough Castle
Tel: 01423 556188. Open Easter–Sep daily.
Marmion Tower
West Tanfield, Ripon. Medieval gatehouse with fine oriel window. Open all year. Free.

Mother Shipton's Cave
Knaresborough. Tel: 01423 864600. Open all year daily, except Christmas Day.

Nidderdale Museum
Council Offices, Pateley Bridge. Tel: 01423 711225. Open Easter–Oct daily; Nov–Easter weekends.

Newby Hall and Gardens
Ripon. Tel: 01423 322583. Gobelin tapestries and a collection of sculptures are among the attractions at this late 17th-century house with interiors designed by Robert Adam. Open Apr–Sep, most days.

Norton Conyers
Ripon. Tel: 01765 640333. Occupied by the Graham family since 1624. Open house and garden: Easter to mid-Sep on certain days.

Old Courthouse Museum
Castle Yard, Knaresborough. Tel: 01423 869274. Open Easter and May–Sep daily.

Ripley Castle
Ripley. Tel: 01423 770152. Home of the Ingilby family since 1320. The National Collection of Hyacinths and the Ripley Tropical Plant Collection can be seen in the gardens. House open certain days in Apr, May & Oct; daily Jun, Jul & Aug. Gardens open certain days in Mar, Apr–Dec daily.

Ripon Prison and Police Museum
St Mary's Gate. Tel: 01765 690799. History of law and order and the penal system over the last 100 years in Ripon, illustrated by prints, documents and memorabilia, housed in a late 17th-century prison. Open Apr–Oct, most days.

Royal Pump Room Museum
Royal Parade, Harrogate. Tel: 01423 556188. Open all year, closed Mon (except Bank Hols), Christmas and New Year.

Stump Cross Caverns
Between Pateley Bridge and Grassington. On B6265 west of Pateley Bridge. Tel: 01756 752780. Open Apr–Oct daily, Nov–Mar weekends.

Yorkshire Country Wines
Riverside Cellars, The Mill, Glasshouses, Harrogate. Tel: 01423 711947/711223. Open Wed–Sun in season; weekends only Christmas to Easter. Guided tours Fri and Sat.

SPECIAL INTEREST FOR CHILDREN

The following places may be of interest to visitors with children. Unless otherwise stated there will be an admission charge.

Lightwater Valley Theme Park and Village
North Stainley. Tel: 01765 635368. Rides and attractions suitable for all the family, boating lake and children's visitor farm. Open Jun–Aug daily, Apr, May, Sep & Oct weekends only.

Ripley Castle
Ripley. Tel: 01423 770152. Home of the Ingilby family since 1320, its gardens are home to the National Collection of Hyacinths and the Ripley Tropical Plant Collection. House open certain days in Apr, May, & Oct, daily Jun, Jul & Aug. Gardens open certain days Mar, Apr–Dec daily.

Ripon Prison and Police Museum
St Mary's Gate. Tel: 01765 690799. The history of law and order and the penal system over the last 100 years in Ripon illustrated by prints, documents and memorabilia housed in a late 17th-century prison. Open Apr–Oct, most days.

Stump Cross Caverns
Between Pateley Bridge and Grassington. On B6265 west of Pateley Bridge. Tel: 01756 752780. Open Apr–Oct daily, Nov–Mar weekends.

Shopping

Harrogate
Large shopping centre and mall, including the Victoria Shopping Centre. Harrogate is especially good for antiques and second-hand books.

Knaresborough
Open-air market, Wed.

Ripon
The Lightwater Village, which is next to Lightwater Valley Theme Park, is a shopping centre with factory outlets. Open-air market, Thu.

LOCAL SPECIALITIES

Craft workshops
King Street Workshop, King Street, Pateley Bridge. Tel: 01423 712570. Several craft workshops, including pottery, jewellery and glassblowing. Opening hours vary.

Glass
Richard Bray Glass Engraving Studio, Brimham Rocks Farm, Summerbridge. Tel: 01423 780786. Displays of glassware and crystals, hand-engraving and sculptures. Open daily, check at weekends.

Pottery
Littlethorpe Potteries, Littlethorpe, Ripon. Tel: 01765 603786. Country pottery using local clay, with pot throwing demonstrations. Open all year daily.

Wood products
David Bailes Woodworking, Finkle Street, Knaresborough. Tel: 01423 868438. Clocks.

The Performing Arts

Harrogate Theatre
Oxford Street, Harrogate. Tel: 01423 502116.

Sports, Activities and the Outdoors

ANGLING

Fly
Pateley Bridge Scar House Dam. Day tickets from Lofthouse Post Office. Tel: 01423 755203.

BOAT HIRE

Knaresborough
Blenkhowns Boat Hire, 6 Waterside, High Bridge. Tel: 01423 862105. Rowing boats, punts and canoes for hire.

GOLF COURSES

Harrogate
Crimple Valley Golf Club, Hookstone Wood Road. Tel: 01423 883485.
Harrogate Golf Club, Forest Lane Head. Tel: 01423 862999.
Oakdale Golf Club, off Kent

Road. Tel: 01423 567162.
Pannal Golf Club, Follifoot Road.
Tel: 01423 872628.
Rudding Park Golf Club,
Rudding Lane, Follifoot.
Tel: 01423 872100.

Knaresborough
Knaresborough Golf Club,
Boroughbridge Road. Tel: 01423
862690.

Ripon
Ripon City Golf Club, Palace
Road. Tel: 01765 603640.

GOLF DRIVING RANGE

Knaresborough
Scotton Golf Driving Range,
Lingerfield. Tel: 01423 868943.

HORSE-RACING

Ripon
2 miles (3.2km) southeast of
Ripon on B6265. Tel: 01765
602156.

HORSE-RIDING

Ripon
Swinton Riding and Trekking
Centre.
Tel: 01765 689636.

LONG-DISTANCE
FOOTPATHS AND TRAILS

The Ridge Walk
A 20-mile (32-km) moorland
circuit around Upper

Nidderdale, starting at
Middlesmoor.
The Upper Nidderdale Way
A 23-mile (36.8-km) walk from
Pateley Bridge to Kettlewell.

Annual Events and Customs

Fountains Abbey
Egg-rolling, Easter Monday.
Harrogate
Harrogate International Youth
Music Festival, held every Easter,
with performances throughout
the region including Ripon
Cathedral.
Spring Flower Show, late April.
The Great Yorkshire Show, mid-
July.
Harrogate International Festival,
late July to early August.
Trans-Pennine Run for vintage
vehicles from Manchester to
Harrogate, early August.
Autumn Flower Show, mid-
September.
Northern Antiques Show, late
September.
Knaresborough
Knaresborough Bed Race, early
June, charity race around town
and across the river.
Knaresborough Charter Day,
mid-August, celebrates the 1310
market charter.

Middlesmoor
Bell Festival, June.
Pateley Bridge
Nidderdale Show late
September, held in Bewerley
Park.
Ripley
Craft shows at the castle each
Spring and Summer Bank
Holiday.
Ripon
Setting the Watch by the Ripon
Hornblower every evening in the
market place by the Obelisk at
9pm, 1100-year-old tradition.
Every Thursday at 11am the
Ripon Bellringer declares the
market open.
Ripon Charter Festival, late May
to early June.
St Wilfrid's Feast Procession,
Saturday before the first Monday
in August.

The checklists give details of just
some of the facilities within the
area covered by this guide.
Further information can be
obtained from Tourist
Information Centres.

*Harrogate prides itself on its
floral displays*

The Central Dales

This is the heart of the Dales. It has the highest peaks – Ingleborough, Whernside, Pen-y-ghent and Buckden Pike – the biggest caverns, including the exciting White Scar Caves, potholes galore and attractive villages and towns, little-touched, it seems, by the worst aspects of modern times. It is a landscape both rolling and rugged, a landscape for walkers, for climbers, for cavers and for fell runners – those who like their scenery to have a challenge about it. But it also has much to offer less energetic visitors, who are content to marvel at the grandeur of it all from lesser altitudes.

THE NORBER BOULDERS
Follow the bridleway between Clapham and Austwick and you will see a signpost to the Norber Boulders. This scattering of boulders, each on its own little pedestal of rock, at first glance looks as if it ought to be of some human significance, but in fact is a natural occurrence. The boulders, also called the Norber Erratics, are several hundred million years old and were deposited in their present location by the actions of a glacier about 25,000 years ago. They are made of Silurian gritstone, the type of rock found in Crummack Dale about half a mile (800m) to the north.

CLAPHAM North Yorkshire Map ref SD7469
Clapham is one of the prettiest little villages that anyone could wish to find; it is almost as if it was planned with the picture postcard in mind. A stream runs through its centre, crossed by old stone bridges, and matching old stone cottages line its narrow lanes. It is much more wooded than most villages in the Dales, which adds to its appeal, and with several guesthouses and cafés, a pub, a National Park Centre with displays and an information service, a nature trail and a few shops for essential supplies, it makes an excellent base for exploring the southern part of this area.

The Ingleborough Estate Nature Trail celebrates one of Clapham's sons, Reginald Farrer, who travelled the world collecting plant species and cultivated them here, on the family estate. He died in 1920, before he was 40, but by that time he had become one of Britain's leading botanical experts and earned himself the name of 'the father of English rock gardening'. The trail also leads to Ingleborough Cave, where guided tours of almost an hour take visitors into the network of caves below Ingleborough, which include what is said to be the longest stalactite in the country, at 5 feet (1.5m).

For such a small place, Clapham has several claims to fame. The caves have been open to visitors since 1838, when a stalagmite barrier about 70ft (20m) in was first breached giving access to the labyrinthine network beyond. Modern cave diving techniques have allowed underground links to be made as far as Gaping Gill (see page 64). A past Clapham man was James Faraday, the village blacksmith and father of Michael Faraday, the great physicist and chemist who formulated Faraday's Law on electrolysis and whose discoveries led to the invention of the dynamo, the electric motor and refrigeration.

GRASSINGTON   North Yorkshire Map ref SE0063
Grassington may look as if it has always been a small and sleepy Dales town, but this is certainly not the case. With the discovery of large lead deposits on the surrounding moors, it became a thriving industrial town from the 17th to the 19th centuries, so much so that by the early 1800s it was noted for its drunken and violent nature. The arrival of Methodism did much to improve matters, and two large Georgian-style chapels still survive in the village, though one is now a Congregational church.

Modern Grassington is the main tourist centre in Upper Wharfedale, with any number of guesthouses, shops and eating places radiating out from its cobbled market square. It also has a National Park Centre, and the Upper Wharfedale Folk Museum, a tiny but enjoyable collection housed in two 18th-century former lead-miners' cottages. Five miles (8km) southeast, off the B6160, is Appletreewick, where the Parcevall Hall Gardens offer woodland walks, orchards, a 15th-century farmhouse and wonderful views of Wharfedale.

THE WITCH OF CLAPHAM
Dame Alice Ketyll, a Clapham inhabitant in the mid-15th century, was an unusual witch in that she was popular with the villagers, using her mysterious powers for their benefit wherever possible. She was less popular with the Church – an ecclesiastical court tried her for witchcraft and punished her by demanding that she line the roof of the village church with lead. Dame Alice could not afford to buy the lead, so she took a party of clerics and workmen to Ingleborough where they found both lead and silver. The silver paid the men to take the lead and line the church roof, and Dame Alice's reward for this ingenuity was that she could be buried in the churchyard.

A shady beck flows through the centre of Clapham

Flags adorn the buildings lining Grassington's cobbled Market Square

BRITAIN'S WILD WEST

Close to the Ribblehead Viaduct are a few trenches which are all that remain of Batty Green. This was the name given to the village of wooden huts which housed up to 2,000 workmen in the 1870s, when they were working on the remarkable Settle–Carlisle railway line. There are interpretative panels by the site and a further display in the staion. Batty Green and other shanty towns were Britain's own Wild West in Victorian times, with saloons, religious missions, good-time girls and fearsome reputations.

Six miles (9.6km) southeast of Grassington on the B6160, is Barden Tower, a medieval hunting lodge which was renovated and used by the redoubtable Lady Anne Clifford in the mid-17th century. Lady Anne was an admirable woman whose name you will encounter throughout the Dales. Her father was the Earl of Cumberland, who died when Anne was only 15, but instead of inheriting his estate as the Earl's only child, she discovered that he had bequeathed it all, including his vast lands in Cumberland, Westmorland and Yorkshire, to his brother and then to his brother's son. Lady Anne fought all her life to regain her inheritance, which she eventually did when her cousin died without heirs. She put her wealth to good use, renovating many buildings, including Barden Tower and she lived there from 1657 until her death in 1676 at the age of 86. The Lady Anne Clifford Trail was established in 1990 to commemorate the 400th anniversary of her birth in Skipton Castle, where the trail begins.

HORTON IN RIBBLESDALE North Yorkshire
Map ref SD8071

The kind of village which straggles alongside a main road, Horton is easily missed but is an important place for many visitors to the Dales. It sits surrounded by the Dales' Three Peaks of Pen-y-ghent, Whernside and Ingleborough, and the Three Peaks Challenge Race starts and ends in Horton every year. The Pen-y-ghent Café has become an important centre for walkers, particularly for the safety system it operates, allowing you to clock out and clock back in again at the end of the day.

The Pennine Way weaves through the village, which also has a station on the Settle–Carlisle line. A big attraction near by is the Ribblehead Viaduct, one of the railway's major achievements, with 24 arches rising to 165 feet (50m) above the valley floor.

HUBBERHOLME North Yorkshire Map ref SD9278

With its riverside setting, surrounded by trees in the valley floor, there can be fewer more picturesque places than Hubberholme. It is not surprising, then, to discover that it was the favourite place of J B Priestley. This Bradford author, who wrote *The Good Companions* and many other books and stage plays, loved Hubberholme and visited it often. He drank in the village pub, and a plaque in the church commemorates his affection for the tiny place where his ashes are now scattered.

Its Church of St Michael and All Angels was originally a Forest chapel and is one of the delights of the Dales. A major attraction is its rood loft from 1558, which only survives thanks to Hubberholme's isolation. In 1571 an edict was issued in the York Diocese to destroy all rood lofts in the region, but Hubberholme's was one of only two in Yorkshire to escape the destruction. Look also for the mouse symbol of Robert Thompson, the 'Mouseman', who made much of the church's more recent woodwork. The work of this Yorkshire furniture maker is distinguished by a tiny mouse carved somewhere on the piece.

THE HUBBERHOLME PARLIAMENT

Behind the George Inn in Hubberholme is a field owned by the church which is known as the 'poor pasture'. On the first Monday in January, after a church service, the 'Hubberholme Parliament' sits in the George. The public bar is the Commons, where the farmers sit, and the lounge bar the Lords, where the church wardens sit with the vicar, who acts as auctioneer. The farmers bid to rent the pasture for one year, the money going to help the sick and poor of the parish. It is what is known as a 'candle auction', lasting for as long as a candle, lit at 8pm, will burn. The Hubberholme candle usually lasts till about midnight, at which point the bidding gets serious among the farmers who genuinely do want the land for grazing.

Hubberholme's church features a magnificent 16th-century oak rood loft

Limestone pavements beneath the plateau of Ingleborough, one of Yorkshire's famous Three Peaks

THE THREE PEAKS RACE

First completed in 1887, this walk traditionally starts in late April each year at the Pen-y-ghent Café in Horton in Ribblesdale, where a safety system of checking everyone in and out operates. The route takes walkers to the top of Ingleborough, Whernside and Pen-y-ghent. That first walk took ten hours, although anyone who completes the 25-mile (40.2km) route in under 12 hours is eligible to join the Three Peaks of Yorkshire Club. If an average speed of only 2mph (3.5kph) doesn't seem very high, remember that the total height of the Three Peaks, each of which must be ascended on the walk, is over 7,000 feet (2,150m), and so it is not a challenge to be undertaken lightly.

INGLEBOROUGH North Yorkshire
Map ref SD7494

There are several ways of approaching Ingleborough on foot, from Clapham, Ingleton, Horton and Chapel-le-Dale, and each is an invigorating but rewarding climb to the top of the peak's 2,373 feet (723m). Until the accurate measurement of hills became possible, Ingleborough was long believed to be the highest point in Yorkshire. We now know that it is surpassed by both Whernside and Mickle Fell. At its top is a wide plateau, with a triangulation point and a stone windbreak, and of course grand views all around. An Iron-Age fort once stood here, and horse races have been run in more recent memory, with bonfires still lit occasionally for special celebrations.

The path from Chapel-le-Dale is the shortest and the steepest approach, giving a daunting impression of the challenge to come as you look up at Ingleborough's imposing heights. From Clapham the walk is about 4 miles (6.4km) one-way, passing Ingleborough Cave on the way. Ingleborough's slopes have a great number of potholes, so take care if you stray from the path. Anywhere that is fenced off will be fenced off for a purpose, so don't let curiosity get the better of you.

South of the summit of Ingleborough is the famous Gaping Gill pothole, though to describe it as a pothole is like calling Westminster Abbey a parish church. In fact you could probably fit the abbey inside Gaping Gill: someone has certainly worked out that you can fit York Minster inside the main cavern. This is about 120 feet (37m) high and 500 feet (152m) long, and down into it from the surface the stream of Fell Beck plunges, making it one of the highest waterfalls in Britain at 364 feet (111m). The breathtaking sight of the interior of Gaping Gill is normally reserved for experienced potholers, but twice a year, on Spring and Summer Bank Holidays, local caving clubs set up a winch and bosun's chair and allow members of the public to share the experience.

INGLETON   North Yorkshire Map ref SD6973

Ingleton has too much modern sprawl to be called a pretty village, but it has an attractive centre with steep winding streets going down to the gorge where its celebrated Waterfalls Walk starts. Before the railway arrived in the late 19th century, bringing the visitors who heralded much of the new development, Ingleton relied on its wool- and cotton-spinning industries, and before that coal-mining quarrying. Now instead of mill-workers' cottages there are guesthouses, gift shops and several good pubs, though the nearby crushed rock quarry is still one of the largest in the Dales.

Its Church of St Mary the Virgin is in a dominating position, and has been rebuilt several times over the centuries, though its 15th-century tower remains. Its oldest feature is the Norman font, carved with figures from the life of Christ, which was rediscovered in 1830, having been hidden in the river below for safe-keeping during times of religious persecution. The church also boasts what is known as the 'Vinegar Bible', so-called because of a misprint in what should have been the Parable of the Vineyards.

On the B6255 to the northeast of Ingleton are the White Scar Caves, the best show caves in the Dales. With underground rivers and waterfalls, these make for an exciting trip underground on one of the guided tours.

RAILWAY (DIS)CONNECTIONS

The railway reached Ingleton in 1849, and 11 years later the viaduct was built to link the Skipton–Ingleton line with the Ingleton–Carlisle line. Unfortunately, the two railway companies which ran the two different lines were involved in a dispute at the time, and a station had to be built at either end of the viaduct. Any passengers making the full journey had to walk from one end to the other in order to board the rival company's service. This only lasted a year, though, and afterwards trains were allowed to make the full journey each way.

St Mary's at Ingleton boasts a splendid carved Norman font

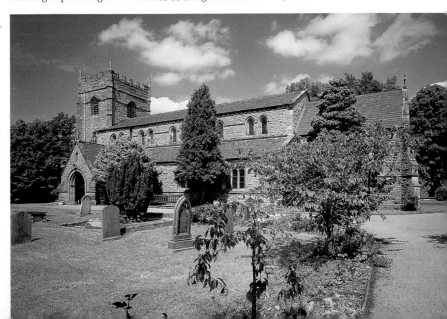

The Ingleton Glens and Waterfalls

One of the best walks in the Dales, taking in glens and numerous impressive falls. Although the route follows mostly man-made pathways, it is lengthy and can be slippery, so boots should be worn. Best walked in the spring for the flowers, trees and birds.

Time: 3 hours. Distance: 4½ miles (7.2km).
Location: In Ingleton.
Start: Follow the signs in Ingleton for Waterfalls Walk and park in the official car park at the start of the walk.
(OS grid ref: SD693734.) Note: The walk is on private land and an entrance fee is charged.
OS Map: Outdoor Leisure 2
(Yorkshire Dales – Southern & Western areas) 1:25,000.
See Key to Walks on page 121.

A torrent of brackish water pours down from the hills at Thornton Dale

ROUTE DIRECTIONS

From the car park in **Ingleton** walk through the picnic area and follow the single man-made path by the River Twiss to view the falls. Take care as spray from the falls can make the paths wet, and lives have been lost through people straying from the official path.

Pass through Swilla Glen, with its high limestone walls and rich woodland. Here the river has wide pools and short sets of rapids. At quiet times, such as early morning, **wildlife** may be seen here. Cross the river twice by the footbridges to the impressive **Pecca Falls**. The path continues on past a refreshment hut up to **Thornton Force**, which comes into view on your right. These falls, 46 feet (14m) high, are a wide curtain of water after heavy rain. From above the falls enjoy the splendid view back towards Ingleton.

The path swings left then right over a bridge across the river. Go up to a gate, then turn right down a grassy lane with beautiful views over swathes of green pasture. Go through two gates, passing farm buildings on your right. Go over a stile by a third gate and keep straight on. Follow the path with views across to White Scar Cave and Ingleton Quarry and continue down to the gate in the wall.

Cross the road and go down the lane turning right through two gates and through a farmyard, turn left and continue with the River Doe on your left. Follow the path passing splendid falls and gorges, pass through a gate and head back through old quarry workings towards Ingleton. The footpath meets a residential road, which you follow into the town. At the main road, turn right and continue through the town, crossing the river by turning right below the church. Turn right again to return to the car park and the start of the walk.

POINTS OF INTEREST

Ingleton

Ingleton has a Tourist Information Centre and an interesting church. The Church of St Mary has a Norman font and a so-called 'Vinegar Bible', in which a misprint shows the Parable of the Vineyards as the Parable of the Vinegar.

History of the Walk

It is hard to believe that these falls were not discovered until the 19th century, as Ingleton had been renowned for its caves and splendid scenery for a hundred years before. In the late 19th century it was decided to make them accessible to the public. The walk was opened in 1885 and by 1888 almost 4,000 people were visiting the falls daily at the height of the season, paying one penny each for the privilege.

Wildlife

The woods near the start of the walk are home to deer, and birds which may be seen here include herons, tawny owls and woodpeckers. Conditions in the damp woodlands are ideal for fungi such as velvet shank and deadman's finger, and also for lichen.

Pecca Falls

Your first glimpse is deceptive, showing you only the first few falls of the five

that make up this sequence. The last fall you reach is a thunderous plunge whose spray fills the air some 30 or 40 yards (27–36m) away. Some pools are believed to be as deep as the falls themselves are high.

Thornton Force

The upper part of the rocks behind the falls is limestone, the lower part is slate. About 300 million years ago, at the start of the Carboniferous Period, a warm sea flowed in over the mountains around here, depositing the limestone. The pebbles and rocks beneath the falls represent the site of the beach.

The tawny owl is part of the rich and varied wildlife of Swilla Glen

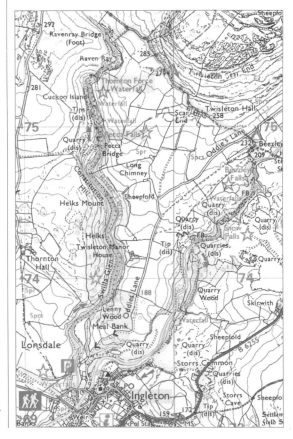

WATER BABIES

Charles Kingsley, author of *The Water Babies* and *Westward Ho!*, visited the Dales on several occasions. He stayed in the village of Arncliffe, just west of Kettlewell, and also at Malham Tarn. A section of *The Water Babies*, where Tom the chimney sweep escapes over some limestone terraces, describes Littondale, in which Arncliffe stands.

KETTLEWELL North Yorkshire Map ref SD9772

Because the main Wharfedale road scarcely touches the village, much of Kettlewell remains a quiet retreat of charming 17th- and 18th-century houses. It was once much more important than it is today, as it was given a market charter in the 13th century, and Fountains Abbey, Bolton Priory and Coverham Abbey all owned tracts of land near by. Later there were flourishing lead-mining and local textile industries too, which helped create those charming houses.

Kettlewell's past is full of interesting stories. In 1218 its parson was murdered, the deed believed to have been done by a man who had taken the parson's mistress and stolen her away to Skipton. A later parson turned part of his house into an inn, to help supplement his meagre stipend.

When abbeys such as Fountains and Jervaulx were at their prime, they owned vast amounts of Dales land, much of it used for grazing their sheep. They built granges in some of the further places, as bases, and these were connected with the abbey by the equivalent of a drovers' road, allowing large flocks of sheep to be moved. Many of these are still in use as paths and bridleways, an excellent example being Mastiles Lane, which runs from Malham, across Mastiles and Kilnsey Moor, to emerge at the Wharfe near Kilnsey. Kilnsey Hall, now in a sorry state of repair, was once a grange for Fountains Abbey. Part of the walk on page 72 is along Mastiles Lane.

Great Whernside looms above the bustling village of Kettlewell

Kilnsey Crag, a bulbous limestone bulge that looms ominously towards the main road, attracts climbers and film-makers in equal numbers. It stands 170 feet (52m) high, with a 40-foot (12m) overhang. Near by is Kilnsey Park, with trout-fishing ponds, nature displays, an aquarium, pot-bellied pigs, picnic area, playground and farm shop.

Kettlewell is a good base for walking – the Dales Way passes right through the village, whereas the traffic passes by. Walkers make full use of its guesthouses and pubs after days spent exploring the riverside paths, the moors and the minor Dales near by. A popular route is to take a path heading south over Knipe Scar and then head along the River Skirfare and up the lesser-known but delightful Littondale with 2,000-foot (610m) hills on either side of the valley.

KIRKBY LONSDALE Cumbria Map ref SD6178

This tiny market town stands just over the border in Cumbria and marks the far western limit of the Yorkshire Dales. Indeed, some guides to the region exclude it altogether, as do guides to the Lake District further north, giving it something of the air of the town that time forgot. It is a delightfully unspoilt place, whose charms have been recognised by artists and authors over the years, from Constable and Turner to Ruskin and Wordsworth, all of whom have sung its praises in no small measure.

RUSKIN'S VIEW

In his 1810 *Guide to the Lakes*, William Wordsworth ventured as far as Kirkby Lonsdale, on the very edge of the Yorkshire Dales, and advised readers: 'By no means omit looking at the Vale of Lune from the Churchyard'. Eight years later, the artist Turner immortalised that same view in a watercolour entitled *Kirkby Lonsdale Churchyard*. (Turner stayed, incidentally, at the Sun Hotel, still standing in Market Street.) Later still, the writer and art critic John Ruskin referred to this setting as: 'One of the loveliest scenes in England'. He also said that, 'I do not know in all my own country, still less in France or Italy, a place more naturally divine'.

Enjoy the sweeping outlook from Ruskin's View

DOMESDAY

In the Domesday Book, Kirkby Lonsdale is listed as 'Cherchebi', meaning 'a village within a church'. There is no trace now of any Saxon Church – the present Church of St Mary the Virgin is Norman. The word Kirkby, found also at Kirkby Stephen and Kirkby Malham, is here derived either from the Danish Kirk-by (church village) or the Norse Kirkja Byr (church farm). Lonsdale is a modernisation of Lunderdale, the Dale of the Lune.

The market place with its unusual butter cross is the hub of activity in Kirkby Lonsdale

A Roman fort has been excavated at Burrow, 2 miles (3.2km) south of the town, and in 1227 the market charter was granted by Henry III to John de Kirkeby in Lounesdale, which allowed not just for a weekly market but also an annual fair. The fair died out in the 19th century, but the market still thrives every Thursday in the Market Place. Here the butter cross is not ancient but modern – from the early 20th century. The importance of the old market is shown by the many street names which grew up around it: Market Street, Horse Market, Swine Market.

A street which should be seen is Mill Brow, a steep street of stone buildings which leads down to the river. Down the centre, at one time, ran a stream which not only provided the town's drinking water but was also used to power no less than seven mills.

The Church of St Mary the Virgin is a most impressive building. It is thought to date from the late 11th and early 12th centuries, and a Norman archway beneath the solid square tower is a beautiful construction. It has some fine stained glass and a delicately-carved pulpit. Outside, near the north entrance, is a tower which can be clearly seen in Turner's painting of 1822, *Kirkby Lonsdale Churchyard*, another reminder of the timeless nature of this attractive little town with its charming street names such as Salt Pie Lane and Jingling Lane.

Across the River Lune is one of the town's most notable features. The Devil's Bridge, a scheduled Ancient Monument, is a medieval bridge with three graceful arches striding confidently over the water. Its date is not known for sure, though records from the late 14th century tell of repairs to a bridge in the town. Nor is it known when it first acquired its cheerful name, although a poem of 1821 tells the tale. A Yorkshire woman, known for being a cheat, one night heard her cow and pony calling from the far side of the swollen river. The devil appeared and offered to build her a bridge, and his payment would be to keep the first thing that crossed over the bridge. Expecting to receive the cow and pony, he was tricked by the canny woman who threw a bun across the bridge, which her dog chased after. The devil grinned at the woman's trickery, and disappeared in flames. The bridge is now open for pedestrians only, to help preserve it. A short way down the river is a piece of limestone through which a hole has been worn by the action of the water. This is affectionately known as the Devil's Neck Collar.

The tall arches of the Devil's Bridge span the inky waters of the Lune

RADICAL STEPS
The Radical Steps, which lead down to the river near Ruskin's View, were built in 1829 by Dr Francis Pearson. They allowed people access to the river, without having to trespass on Dr Pearson's land, which the public footpath crossed before he had it diverted in 1820. The steps gained their name from Dr Pearson's radical views.

From Conistone to Kilnsey Crag

This is an easy stroll through Wharfedale fields which are dominated by the imposing face of Kilnsey Crag. A spring or summer walk, for the best views with clear blue skies.

Time: 1 hour. Distance: 2½ miles (4km).
Location: Conistone is 3 miles (4.8km) south of Kettlewell off the B6160.
Start: Park opposite Conistone Hostel and Chapel. (OS grid ref: SD982674.)
OS Map: Outdoor Leisure 2
(Yorkshire Dales – Southern & Western areas) 1:25,000.
See Key to Walks on page 121.

ROUTE DIRECTIONS

In **Conistone** turn left from the car park and follow the road out of the village towards the B6160. Cross Conistone Bridge then immediately cross the road and take the footpath on the right signed 'Scar Lathe'. There is no mistaking **Kilnsey Crag**, which, at this part of the walk is ahead, slightly to your left, and dominates the landscape. The path takes you almost straight ahead, veering slightly left to the point where the wall turns. Now go ahead with this wall on your left. Scar Lathe is the solitary grey building visible below Kilnsey Crag. When the wall ends head to the left, directly towards this building. Go over a stile in a fence and continue ahead on the path. Note the views of the wide-open valley of Wharfedale to the north. When you reach the building, walk round the far side where to the right there is a gate and a stile.

Cross the stile on to the B6160, turn left and continue

the short distance to the Tennant Arms. At the pub take the right turn marked 'Unsuitable for Motors'. Another road joins from the left; pass this and keep on upwards through **Kilnsey**; the road swings left and continues uphill. As the road flattens, there are lovely views back towards Kilnsey and Conistone, and Wharfedale in all its glory. Bear left on to the wide bridleway signposted 'Malham'. The escarpment is to your right and ahead of you is Cool Scar. Go through a metal gate and 100 yards (91m) beyond this, where the wall on your left turns left at a 90° angle, look for a small wooden gate above the wall which leads over a stile, taking you almost back on yourself.

Walk towards a derelict building, beside which is a lovely little stone footbridge over a stream. Cross this and go through a gate to meet a track coming down from the right. Go over a stile on to the track which leads you down by a stream and back to the

road, passing a farm and emerging alongside a house. Turn left on to the B6160 and then take the first right to cross the bridge and return to Conistone. Take the right turn back to your car.

Alternatively, keep on the B6160 for about 150 yards (137m) and visit the **Kilnsey Park Centre** which, in addition to its other attractions, has a small restaurant. This may be of interest as there is no café or shop in Conistone.

POINTS OF INTEREST

Conistone
Conistone village appears in the Domesday Book as Cunestune, and its farmhouses date from the late 17th century. The attractive village houses are built of local limestone dressed with sandstone. The Church of St Mary is well worth a visit. Inside the church gate on the left is a memorial stone to six young cavers whose bodies lie buried in Mossdale Caverns, where they were lost. The church itself is considered to be one of the oldest buildings in the Craven district, with parts believed to date from Saxon times, though it is largely Norman and was restored in 1846.

Kilnsey Crag
This limestone crag is not particularly high – no match for Great Whernside further up the Dale – but its menacing shape reaching out towards the road is certainly eye-catching. It has caught the eye of film-makers, featuring in the TV series *Emmerdale* and Barbara Taylor Bradford's *A Woman of Substance*. Kilnsey Crag is also the finishing point for the annual August Bank Holiday Fell Race.

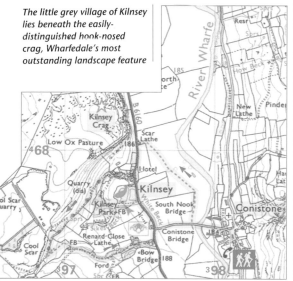

The little grey village of Kilnsey lies beneath the easily-distinguished hook-nosed crag, Wharfedale's most outstanding landscape feature

Kilnsey
In the 12th century the village of Kilnsey belonged to Fountains Abbey, and subsequently became a comparatively industrial village of corn and textile mills. The remains of some of the mills can still be seen.

Kilnsey Park Centre
The centre is devoted to all aspects of rural life, particularly wildlife. Attractions include ducks and fish which children may feed, a museum, aquarium, an adventure playground, accommodation and a restaurant. There are displays of local crafts, such as drystone walling, and facilities for fishing.

THE PENNINE WAY

Britain's first long-distance footpath is the ultimate challenge for many walkers. Its 256 miles (412km) from Derbyshire to Scotland includes a 60-mile (97km) stretch in the Yorkshire Dales, entering, as does this book, near Keighley, and leaving past the lonely Tan Hill Inn, where Yorkshire gives way to County Durham. One of the walk's main instigators was Tom Stephenson, secretary of the Ramblers' Association at the time, and 2,000 ramblers attended the official opening on 24 April 1965 on Malham Moor. Though the route near Pen-y-ghent gives a rugged climb over moorland scarred by caves and potholes, there are many easier and more low-lying stretches, such as along Airedale, south of Malham (see Walk on page 32), all well signposted.

Drystone walling underlines Pen-y-ghent, one of the famous Three Peaks

PEN-Y-GHENT North Yorkshire Map ref SD8373

The lowest but not the least of this region's Three Peaks, Pen-y-ghent in profile seems to be thrusting a jaw out defiantly as if challenging anyone to climb to the top of its 2,277 feet (694m). In its capacity as the third highest of the Three Peaks, many people assume it is the third highest peak in the Yorkshire Dales. This honour, in fact, goes to Buckden Pike, which is 25 feet (8m) higher than Pen-y-ghent! Buckden Pike is 10 miles (16km) away across in Wharfedale, though, so even the fit fell runners would have to think twice about turning the Three Peaks Race into a Four Peaks Race.

Ironically for this most distinctive of Yorkshire's hills, Pen-y-ghent carries a Celtic name, meaning 'hill of the border', once marking the edge of one of the British tribes' kingdoms. For those who want to tackle its challenge, the most common route is a 3-mile (4.8-km) hike from Horton village, following the signs for the Pennine Way, which passes right over the top of the hill.

At the end of the track out of Horton, just beyond the point where the route turns sharp right towards the hill, there are two potholes. The larger is the huge gaping hole known as Hull Pot, into which Hull Pot Beck disappears. Walkers should treat these potholes with extreme caution.

The climb up to the summit of Pen-y-ghent is steep in places, with a little bit of scrambling, but not beyond the capabilities of anyone who is reasonably fit. Once up there, walkers can revel in the views across to the other peaks, north across the fells of Langstrothdale Chase, and south over Ribblesdale and Lancashire's Forest of Bowland.

WHERNSIDE North Yorkshire Map ref SD7381
This is the highest point in the Dales, reaching to
2,415 feet (736m). Like Ingleborough and Pen-y-
ghent, it owes its existence to the time when, over
300 million years ago, this part of the world was not a
walker's paradise but a tropical sea. The sea bed
became thick with the shells of dead creatures, and
this eventually became the Great Scar Limestone that
now lies up to 600 feet (183m) thick underneath
much of this part of the Dales, its scale most clearly
visible at Malham Cove. The Great Scar was mostly
buried under sandstones, shales and other limestones
that were deposited by the rivers which drained into
the ancient sea. It is these extra deposits, known as
the Yoredale Series of rocks, which form the tops of
the Three Peaks and cover much else besides in the
Dales.

There are several approaches to Whernside, but the
two most popular are from the Ribblehead Viaduct or
from Chapel-le-Dale. Maps are needed, but the walks
are so popular that much of the land on the way is
being eroded. Visitors are advised to keep to the
official paths, to save further erosion of this dramatic
landscape.

*The Ribblehead Viaduct
strides across to Whernside*

PEREGRINE FALCONS
Watch out in this rugged region
for a possible glimpse of
peregrine falcons. These
beautiful, sleek birds of prey can
attain speeds of well over
100mph (160kph) when diving
in a 'stoop', falling through the
sky with their wings folded back
to attack their prey at high
speed. Britain contains one-
third of the West European
peregrine population and has
an international responsibility
to protect them. Visitors should
be aware that it is illegal to
approach a peregrine's nest,
and a licence is required even
to photograph them – should
you be lucky enough to see one
at close range!

Central Dales

Leisure Information

Places of Interest

Shopping

Sports, Activities

and the Outdoors

Annual Events and Customs

Checklist

Leisure Information

TOURIST INFORMATION CENTRES

Grassington
National Park Centre, Colvend, Hebden Rd. Tel: 01756 752774.
Horton in Ribblesdale
Pen-y-ghent Café. Tel: 01729 860333.
Ingleton
Community Centre Car Park, Ingleton. Tel: 015242 41049.

NATIONAL PARK CENTRES

Clapham
Tel: 015242 51419.
Grassington
Hebden Road. Tel: 01756 752774. Information screens provide a 24-hour service.

OTHER INFORMATION

British Waterways Board Headquarters
Willow Grange, Church Road, Watford. Tel: 01923 226422.
www.british-waterways.org
English Heritage
37 Tanner Row, York. Tel: 01904 601901.
www.english-heritage.org.uk
Environment Agency
21 Park Square South, Leeds. Tel: 0113 244 0191.
www.environment-agency.gov.uk

National Trust
Yorkshire Regional Office: Goddards, 27 Tadcaster Road, Dringhouses, York. Tel: 01904 702021.
www.nationaltrust.org.uk
Parking
There are pay-and-display car parks at most of the National Park Centres, and visitors are encouraged to use them. Traffic congestion is an increasing problem in some villages.
Yorkshire Wildlife Trust
10 Toft Green, York. Tel: 01904 659570.
Weather
The Three Peaks weather report displayed each weekend at Pen-y-ghent Café. Tel: 01729 860333. The café operates a Safety Service for walkers.

ORDNANCE SURVEY MAPS

Landranger 1:50,000 Sheets 97, 98.
Outdoor Leisure 1:25,000 Sheets 2, 30.

Places of Interest

There will be an admission charge at the following places of interest unless otherwise stated.
Ingleborough Cave
Clapham. Tel: 015242 51242. Guided tours of underground

formations, streams, illuminated pools. Open Mar–Oct daily, Nov–Feb weekends only.
Kilnsey Park and Trout Farm
Kilnsey. Tel: 01756 752150. Daleslife Visitor Centre, children's fishery, playground. Open all year, daily.
Parcevall Hall Gardens
Off B625 between Grassington and Pateley Bridge. Tel: 01756 720311. Open Good Fri–Oct, daily.
Upper Wharfedale Folk Museum
Grassington Square, Grassington. Exhibits relating to Upper Wharfedale housed in 18th-century lead-miners' cottages. Open Apr–Sep, daily, afternoons, Oct–Mar weekend afternoons only.
White Scar Caves
On B6255 north of Ingleton. Tel: 015242 41244. Britain's largest display caverns, tours to underground falls and rivers. Open all year, daily (weather permitting).

SPECIAL INTEREST FOR CHILDREN

The following places may be of interest to visitors with children. Unless otherwise stated there will be an admission charge.

Ingleborough Cave

Clapham. Tel: 015242 51242. Guided tours of underground formations, streams and illuminated pools. Open Mar–Oct daily, Nov–Feb wknds only.

Kilnsey Park and Trout Farm

Kilnsey. Tel: 01756 752150. Daleslife Visitor Centre, children's fishery and adventure playground. Open all year, daily.

Upper Wharfedale Folk Museum

Grassington Square, Grassington. Exhibits housed in 18th-century lead miners' cottages. Open Apr–Sep, daily, afternoons only, Oct–Mar weekend afternoons only.

White Scar Caves

On B6255 north of Ingleton. Tel: 015242 41244. Britain's largest display caverns, tours to underground falls and rivers. Open all year daily (weather permitting).

Shopping

Grassington

Several shops sell outdoor clothing, maps, and books about the area.

Ingleton

Open-air market, Fri.

Kirkby Lonsdale

Open-air market, Thu.

LOCAL SPECIALITIES

Crafts

Curlew Crafts, Main Street, Ingleton. Tel: 015242 41608. Pottery, jewellery, walking sticks.

Fossils

The Rock Shop, Main Street, Ingleton. Tel: 015242 42135. Fossils, jewllery and other items.

Outdoor Clothing and Equipment

Daleswear Ltd, Laundry Lane, Ingleton. Tel: 015242 41477. Over and Under, Low Hall, Kettlewell. Tel: 01756 760871. Pen-y-ghent Café, Horton in Ribblesdale. Tel: 01729 860333.

Pottery

Ingleton Pottery, Bank Bottom, Ingleton. Tel: 015242 41363.

Paintings, Prints and Books

The Dales Book Centre, Main Street, Grassington. Tel: 01756 753373.

Sports, Activities and the Outdoors

ANGLING

Fly

Ingleton Six miles (9.7km) of trout fishing on local rivers. Permits are available from Denbighs Newsagents, Main Street, Ingleton. Tel: 015242 41683.

Kilnsey Kilnsey Park Trout Farm. Tel: 01756 752150.

Kirkby Lonsdale Fishing on the River Lune. Weekly and daily permits from Kirkby Lonsdale Tourist Information Centre. Tel: 015242 71437.

Redwell Fishery. On B6254 Carnforth road. Tel: 015242 21979. Day tickets available.

CAVING

Horton in Ribblesdale

Introductory caving trips, some suitable for families, can be booked through Yorkshire Dales Guides, 2 Moughton Villas, Horton in Ribblesdale. Tel: 01729 860357.

CYCLE HIRE

Kettlewell

W R M Wilkinson, The Garage. Tel: 01756 760225.

GOLF COURSES

Casterton

Casterton Golf Club, Sedbergh Road, Casterton. Tel: 015242 71592.

Kirkby Lonsdale

Kirkby Lonsdale Golf Club, Scaleber Lane, Barbon. Tel: 015242 76365.

GUIDED WALKS

Contact the National Park Centre, Colvend, Hebden Road, Grassington. Tel: 01756 752774.

HORSE-RIDING

Kilnsey Trekking and Riding Centre, Homestead Farm, Conistone. Trekking and weekly holidays. Tel: 01756 752861.

LONG-DISTANCE FOOTPATHS AND TRAILS

The Dales Way

An 81-mile (130-km) lowland walk through the heart of the Yorkshire Dales connecting Ilkley in the south with Bowness-on-Windermere in the north.

The Ingleborough Estate Nature Trail

Starts at the National Park Centre at Clapham and leads to Ingleborough Cave.

Annual Events and Customs

Burnsall

Burnsall Feast and Fell Race, early August.

Clapham

Gaping Gill public descents by winch and bosun's chair each Spring and Summer Bank Hol.

Grassington

Grassington Festival, mid-June to early July.

Horton in Ribblesdale

The Three Peaks Race, end April. Horton Gala and Pen-y-ghent Race, June.
Horton in Ribblesdale Show, late September.
Ribblehead Sheep Show, late September.
Annual Three Peaks Cyclo-Cross, late September.

Hubberholme

On New Year's Day the 'Hubberholme Parliament' sits in the George Inn after a church service.

Ingleton

Annual Fellsman Hike, Ingleton to Threshfield, early May.
Gala and mountain race, mid-July.
Horticultural Show, early September.

Kilnsey

The Kilnsey Show, late August.

The checklists give details of just some of the facilities within the area covered by this guide. Further information can be obtained from Tourist Information Centres.

Wensleydale

If there is one dale above all others that people associate with the Yorkshire Dales, it is Wensleydale. It is the longest, running for over 40 miles (64km), and has some of the prettiest landscapes in the region. Where other dales have rugged features, Wensleydale's are more soft and rounded, the slopes of its hills lush and green, its pastures grazed by large flocks of sheep and broken up with long stretches of drystone walls. Its name is also known far and wide because of Wensleydale sheep and Wensleydale cheese.

THE BAINBRIDGE HORNBLOWER

On Askrigg's doorstep is the village of Bainbridge, where, at 9pm each winter evening, a member of the Metcalfe family will stop whatever they are doing and blow three foghorn-like blasts on the old Bainbridge horn. This tradition is believed to go back to Norman times when Wensleydale was one large forest, populated by wolves, and the sound of the horn would guide travellers through the dark to safety. It is said that the horn can be heard 3 miles (4.8km) away, but the Hornblower has a traditional answer, should you ask if this is true: 'I don't know, I'm always at this end.'

Picturesque Askrigg proved popular with millions of TV viewers across the world

ASKRIGG North Yorkshire Map ref SD9491

Though it may only be a small place, Askrigg demonstrates well the ebbs and flows of history. It received its market charter in 1587, but only because Wensley, further down the dale, had been almost wiped out by the plague in 1563. The result was the further decline of Wensley and prosperity for Askrigg, where a number of small local industries blossomed alongside the busy weekly market: clock-making, brewing, spinning and dyeing.

The age of the train brought a downturn to Askrigg's fortunes, as the Wensleydale station was situated at Hawes – less than 3 miles (4.8km) away, but sufficiently distant to ensure the switch to Hawes as the focus of Wensleydale, which it remains to this day. However, when television film-makers were looking for an unspoilt Dales town to represent the fictional Darrowby

in James Herriot's *All Creatures Great and Small*, it was Askrigg that fitted the bill. Now visitors come once more, to see the locations used for filming, and Askrigg flourishes again because of its recent lack of development.

AYSGARTH   North Yorkshire Map ref SE0088

The Aysgarth Falls are not in Aysgarth, but just outside the village centre on the road to Carperby. Visitors need not worry about missing them, though, as this major Wensleydale attraction is well signposted, with a Yorkshire Dales National Park Centre and adjoining car park, and a busy little cluster of shops and cafés catering for the crowds.

The name Aysgarth means an open place marked by oak trees, and as visitors walk through the woods to view the Middle and Lower Falls, few realise that they are strolling through one of the last remnants of the ancient forest of Wensleydale, which once covered most of the countryside here.

There are three sets of falls at Aysgarth – Upper, Middle and Lower – each with their differing attractions, though their appeal lies in the width of the river at this point and visitors must not expect torrents of water tumbling from on high. These falls are gentler, but still extraordinarily beautiful, with the Upper Falls perhaps the best of all. They are on private land and a small

THE GARIBALDI CONNECTION

The buildings around the bridge at Aysgarth Falls once made up Yore Mill, a cotton mill first built in the 1780s. It later became a woollen mill, and burnt down in 1853, only to be rebuilt the following year. It later sold 7,000 shirts to Italy which were used by the troops of General Giuseppe Garibaldi, whose famous red-shirted volunteers conquered Sicily and Naples, which led to the formation of the Italian state in 1861.

Casting a line at Aysgarth's Lower Falls

The foaming waters of the Ure at the Middle Falls are seen at their best after heavy rain

THE HERRIOT CONNECTION
Carperby is still one of the Dales' quieter villages, with an 18th-century market cross and a 19th-century Quaker Meeting House, though fans of the author and vet James Herriot like to visit to see the Wheatsheaf Hotel, in which he and his wife, Helen, spent their honeymoon in the 1930s.

admission charge, by way of an honesty box, has been introduced by the landowner for providing access to the best viewpoints. Some avoid the charge altogether by walking round to view the falls from the road near by and the 18th-century bridge, but the road is both busy and narrow, and its zigzag curve either side of the bridge reduces visibility. Better to pay a small charge than to cause a large accident.

Before heading off to look at the rest of the falls, pick up a walk leaflet from the National Park Centre, which provides some fascinating information about the woods you will be walking through and the local wildlife. On the far side of the bridge from the Upper Falls, the signposted path leads down to the Middle and Lower Falls. This is a pleasant walk through the leafy woodland known as the Freeholders' Wood, but watch out for the side paths through the trees that lead to views of these other falls, which are narrower but with deeper plunges, the Lower Falls being the most impressive. The path is fairly easy as far as the Middle Falls, but becomes trickier underfoot further on as it begins to step down, so elderly visitors or those with young children are advised to take care. It is about a mile (1.6km) from the Upper down to the Lower Falls.

The Freeholders' Wood through which you pass is now being managed by the National Park Authority, though its freeholders are mainly people from the next village, Carperby, who retain certain rights on the land such as the free gathering of firewood.

Around the bridge and car park there are several gift shops, a tea shop, and another popular attraction in the Yorkshire Carriage Museum. This specialist collection is housed in the upstairs rooms of the Yore Mill buildings, which was in operation as a flour mill until 1959. Eight years later the museum took over the premises, and has amassed a fascinating collection of carriages from the horse-drawn to the motorised, by way of hearses, haunted carriages, penny-farthings and other odd bicycles, a fire engine, farm carriages, stage coaches and Irish jaunting cars.

BEDALE North Yorkshire Map ref SE2688

To include Bedale in Wensleydale is stretching a point just a little, as it is in the next valley east of the River Ure, but it is an attractive old market town through which most people will pass if driving from the A1 into Wensleydale. It is worth a stop, though, and a foray into the countryside around.

Bedale gained its market charter in 1251, with a market cross that dates from the 14th century. On the wide main street stands Bedale Hall, a grand Georgian mansion which today serves as impressive council offices. Inside is the Tourist Information Centre and a tiny local museum, the main exhibit here is a fire engine from 1748. The church contains a 400-year-old bell rescued from Jervaulx Abbey after the Dissolution of the Monasteries.

THE ODDFELLOWS ARMS
This Bedale pub, located on Emgate, was built from the original brewery cottages and the adjacent customs house. The bonded cellar from the customs house is still in use, but these days it acts as the pub's wine cellar.

Bedale's Church of St Gregory with its delightful off-centre clock looks down the main street of this little town

Tranquillity reigns at the old Crakehall Watermill

HIT FOR SIX

The village of Thornton Watlass, 2 miles (3.2km) south of Bedale, is an attractive place, the archetypal English village with a large green on which cricket is played in summer. If visiting the village pub, the Buck Inn, when a match is on, take care not to park in front of the building: the pub wall forms part of the boundary!

To the northwest is the Crakehall Watermill, a 17th-century mill which again produces flour, following its restoration in 1980. Visitors may or may not see the mill at work as it is a small family-run operation, and although it is open to visitors on some days, the wheels do not necessarily turn every day. A gift shops sells the flour and country craft items, and the mill has a tea shop too, in a very attractive stream-side setting, with ducks quacking on Crakehall Beck.

To the south of Bedale, off the B6268, is the Thorp Perrow Arboretum, which boasts over 2,000 species of plants and trees in its 85 acres of garden and woodland. These in their turn are set in over 1,000 acres of parkland owned by Sir John Ropner, who now manages the Arboretum created by Colonel Sir Leonard Ropner over a period of almost 50 years. Many of the species are rare in Britain, and some of the oaks on the site are known to date from the time of Henry VIII, when the land was first cultivated. It is a beautiful collection all year round, but especially when bluebells, cherry blossom or the daffodils are in bloom – in one year recently, the staff planted 7,500 daffodil bulbs!

CASTLE BOLTON North Yorkshire Map ref SE0391
Castle Bolton is a one-street village which most people
pass through in order to see Bolton Castle, which was
built at the end of the 14th century and is a fascinating
place. The castle was built by Sir Richard Scrope as an
impressive residence rather than for any defensive
purposes. Documents covering the construction still
survive, and include a licence to crenellate, dated 1379,
and a builders' contract from 1378 which refers to the
construction of the 'Privees'. The facilities have been
modernised since those days!

If you climb to the top of the turrets for the splendid
views, try to imagine the vast tracts of Wensleydale
Forest which covered the region in medieval times. The
Scropes were a Norman family and had been landowners
in Yorkshire since the 12th century. Sir Richard was born
in 1328, became Member of Parliament for the County
of York in 1364 and rose to twice become Chancellor of
the Exchequer. The Castle was completed in 1399 at a
cost of £12,000, which is the equivalent of well over
£1 million today.

The four corner towers which rise to 100 feet (30.5m)
give only a small indication of the grandeur of the
original building. There were eight separate halls, each
with its own set of rooms, acting as independent
household units inside the stately castle walls. Two
kitchens provided for the castle and guests.

AT HER MAJESTY'S PLEASURE
Although Mary, Queen of
Scots was imprisoned at
Bolton Castle, it was not a
case of living a deprived life in
the dungeons. She arrived
with four carts, 20 carriage
horses and 23 saddle horses,
and the following week five
more carts and four more
horses loaded with her
belongings arrived. Records
show that 30 men and six
ladies from her retinue were
also accommodated at the
castle by the Scrope family,
while 20 more of her servants
were billeted in the village at
the Queen's own expense.
One can't help wondering
who was most
inconvenienced by the
imprisonment – captive or
captor?

*Castle Bolton is a massive
edifice built around 1379*

YORKSHIRE IN A NUTSHELL

'Like every good Tyke I had known five things about Yorkshire from birth. First, that Yorkshire (like Caesar's Gaul) was divided into three parts called Ridings, second that there were more acres in Yorkshire than letters in the Bible, thirdly that the Pennines were there to protect us from Lancastrians, fourthly that you can always tell a Yorkshireman but you can't tell him much, and fifthly (and easily most important) that to be eligible to play for Yorkshire County Cricket Club you must be born within the county boundaries. Years later I had to educate my wife in this last matter when I insisted on a holiday being deferred to ensure that our first-born would, if a boy, be eligible to play for his county.'

From *Gumboot Practice: Portrait of a Country Solicitor* by John Francis (Smith Settle, 1989).

THE TERRIBLE KNITTERS OF DENT

Describe a Dent knitter as 'terrible' and he'd (for they were often men) be flattered, as it traditionally meant they were terribly good. Knitting flourished as a cottage industry in Dent, and its story is told in the Dales Countryside Museum in Hawes. There were knitting schools in Dent; many houses had a wooden knitting gallery. Garments would be taken by horse and cart to Kendal, and on to London. For a look at the craft work of a modern knitter, visit the Shop on the Green. And a 'terrible knitter' still lives next door!

Cobbles and whitewash in the pretty village of Dent, opposite

Bolton Castle's most notable resident, albeit unwillingly, was Mary, Queen of Scots, who was imprisoned here in July 1568 for six months. The bedchamber in which she is thought to have stayed can be seen, and has been decorated in appropriate style, as have many other parts of the castle. Tapestries, arms and armour are on display and tableaux give a vivid impression of life in the castle over the years – including the inevitable scary dungeon, a hole in the ground into which prisoners were usually dropped and forgotten about. One arm bone was found down there, still held by an iron manacle.

On the ground floor, off the courtyard, are many of the working places needed for life in the castle to function smoothly and independently: the brew house, the bake house, the meal house, the forge and the threshing floor, for example. On the first floor is the ruined great hall, with the state chamber and guest hall, while up above is a chapel and some monks' cells. Today's facilities at the castle include a gift shop and simple refreshments.

DENT   Cumbria Map ref SD7086

If there were ever a vote for the most attractive village in the Dales, it would hardly be surprising if Dent won first prize. It is a beautiful cluster of whitewashed cottages and cobbled streets nestling in the lush green valley that is Dentdale. This does, of course, mean that it is extremely busy in the holiday season, and is a place perhaps best visited at other times if possible, when it regains its village charm.

Dent is on the Settle–Carlisle railway line and is the highest mainline station in Britain, at 1,150 feet (351m), but if you are planning to travel by train, be warned that the station is about 5 miles (8km) from the village itself. There is only a connecting bus service on Sundays in summer, so visitors will need to arrange a lift or a taxi. When one local was asked why they built the station so far from the village, he bluntly replied: 'Appen they wanted t'put it near t'track'.

This is not to say that Dent, with a permanent population of only a few hundred souls, is a backwater. In fact it boasts a flourishing artistic community, from the modern practitioners of Dent's knitting tradition to painter John Cooke, musician Mike Harding and photographers John and Eliza Forder, whose studio/shop in the village has a range of their sumptuous books on life in the Yorkshire Dales, prints and postcards. On the road to Sedbergh you will find the Dent Crafts Centre, a marvellous display of local and not-so-local arts and crafts, which also has a café and opens as a restaurant on weekend evenings. In Dent itself there are several cafés and pubs, and even a brewery, and there is a choice of accommodation and souvenir shops.

Adam Sedgwick was born in Dent in the Old Parsonage

in 1785, attended the local Grammar School then went on to become Woodwardian Professor of Geology at Cambridge. He retained his connection with Dent, and his distinguished career as a geologist is marked by the pink Shap granite memorial fountain in the main street. This was not always merely a memorial, as it also provided the town's main water supply until the 1920s. In 1985, to commemorate the 200th anniversary of his birth, the National Park Authority created the Adam Sedgwick Geology Trail, near Sedbergh. Leaflets are available at National Park Centres and Tourist Information Centres.

Near to the Sedgwick Stone is St Andrew's Church, which has a Norman doorway, although most of the church was rebuilt in the late 19th century. Inside are some unusual Jacobean box-pews and flooring of Dent marble. Both black and grey marble were quarried near here in the past. The Stone House Marble Works flourished in the 18th and 19th centuries at Arten Gill, south-east of Dent Station, where you will also find the Dent Head Viaduct, yet another of the marvellous constructions on the Settle–Carlisle railway line. Many of the line's stations contain some of the marble that was originally quarried at Dent. In the days when the quarries were working, the knitters were knitting and the mills were weaving, Dentdales population reached almost 2,000 – about three times what it is today.

Adam Sedgwick's memorial fountain, above

The impressive Dent Head Viaduct, below

HARDRAW FORCE North Yorkshire Map ref SD8792

Hardraw is a hamlet that would probably be visited only by those passing through on the Pennine Way if it was not for the existence of Hardraw Force. At 96 feet (29m) it has the longest free drop of any waterfall in England – above ground, at least – and was painted by J M W Turner on his travels through the Dales. Another unusual feature is that to reach it you must pass through the Green Dragon pub, paying a small entrance fee as you do so. The volume of water from the fall is not great, and it is therefore best visited after heavy rain. Those who do not mind a slight splashing can walk round behind the fall, although great care must be taken on the wet rocks. On two occasions, in 1739 and 1881, the falls froze completely to produce an impressive 100-foot (30.5m) icicle.

The Force falls into a pool in a natural amphitheatre, and the acoustics here are such that an annual brass band contest takes place in September, a tradition that goes back to 1885. Past winners include famous names such as the Black Dyke Mills Band and Besses o' the Barn. The contests once included choirs who stood on the ground above the Force and sang with the bands, but this was not a raging success as they were unable to hear each other. The contests died out for a time but were recently revived and are once more a great attraction.

Hardraw Force tumbles into a natural amphitheatre, famous for its acoustic qualities

A BALANCED MEAL

During one of the brass band contests held in Hardraw's natural amphitheatre in Victorian days, the famous acrobat, Blondin, strung a tightrope across the gorge and walked over it, stopping to cook an omelette half-way across.

THE GREEN DRAGON

The pub through which visitors must pass to reach Hardraw Force is worth a look. It is thought that there has been an inn on this same spot for about 750 years, initially as a grange for the monks of Fountains Abbey who grazed their sheep near by.

THE TURNER TRAIL

The artist J M W Turner visited Wensleydale and Swaledale in 1816, and produced a great number of paintings as a result of his trips. At 16 of the sites he painted, or is known to have visited, seats have been erected to enable visitors to enjoy the same stirring views. A leaflet from Tourist Information Centres entitled 'The Turner Trail' lists these places.

Wensleydale was a favourite location for the great landscape painter J M W Turner

HAWES North Yorkshire Map ref SD8789

Hawes is the kind of old-fashioned market town that seems to be sadly disappearing from the British countryside, though there is little sign yet that this thriving centre is set to go the same way. Family businesses make up the main street, and it is certainly the place to stock up on good local produce, especially on the busy Tuesday market day when stalls line the street and the farmers conduct their business at the livestock market along the Leyburn Road – which visitors too should take a look at, for a flavour of farming life in the Dales. It begins early but goes on till late morning, with a chance to inspect the animals in their pens and to watch the fast and furious bidding in the auction room. This important market sells over 12,000 cattle and 100,000 sheep every year. At one time the livestock was sold in the streets, and men were employed to keep the animals out of the shops!

For a taste of fresh Wensleydale cheese, and the chance to watch it being made, head for the Wensleydale Creamery. This factory was first built in 1897 by a local corn merchant, was rescued from closure in 1935 and was recently endangered again when the owners threatened closure. This would have meant the production of Yorkshire's most famous cheese being transferred to Lancashire. Locals rallied, and the result is not only the survival of the factory but a development of it, opening it up to tourists to create a flourishing visitor centre which includes a museum, video display, licensed restaurant, shop, free cheese-tasting and viewing platforms into the works. The best time to see cheese actually being made is between 10.30am and 3pm.

A more conventional museum is the Dales Countryside Museum, in the Station Yard. The arrival of a rail link in 1877 boosted Hawes' fortunes, as the town had only received its market charter in 1700 after Askrigg, and previously Wensley, had been the focal points of Wensleydale. The trains no longer run but Hawes is now well established as the main town of Upper Wensleydale. It is also, at 850 feet (259m) above sea level, one of the highest market towns in England.

The museum (which also contains a Tourist Information Centre and a National Park Centre) is constantly expanding and has first class displays on life in the Dales, particularly on small local industries such as knitting and peat-cutting. Its collection is enhanced by the inclusion of a great deal of Dales material that was donated by the local authors and historians, Marie Hartley and Joan Ingilby. Just across from the Station Yard is the entrance to Outhwaite and Son, rope-makers, where visitors can see how rope is actually produced as well as buy rope products, gardening items and gifts in the shop.

Hawes makes the perfect base for exploring the delights of Upper Wensleydale, with good walking to be had by striding out in any direction. A more leisurely stroll round the town itself and the adjoining village of Gayle to the south (at one time separate from, and more important than, Hawes) should not be missed either.

Hawes is a thriving market town in the best tradition

WENSLEYDALE'S NECK

Hawes is not merely the heart of Wensleydale, it is also its neck. The name derives from the Old Norse word, Hals, meaning a neck, though in this sense it is a neck of land between two sets of hills. The town was originally known as The Hawes, a name still used by some of the older dialect speakers.

TAKE THE HIGH ROAD

Drive south out of Hawes through Gayle, heading for Kettlewell, and you will cross Wether Fell and Fleet Moss Pass, reaching a height of 1,857 feet (566m). This is the highest road in the Yorkshire Dales, and one of the highest in all England.

According to manuscripts, Jervaulx was founded when the first Abbot, John de Kinstan, was travelling from Byland to Fors with twelve monks and became lost. A vision of the Virgin Mary and Child guided them to safety and told them, 'Ye are late of Byland but now of Yorevale'. The River Ure was actually once known as the Jor, and this was its vale; the abbey was originally called Jorvale Abbey, but the name was altered to Jervaulx to conform to a French style of spelling. The Jor later became the Yore (as in the village of Yorebridge), then the Yeure and finally the Ure.

*The extensive ruins of
Jervaulx Abbey are privately
owned*

JERVAULX ABBEY North Yorkshire Map ref SE1786

This Cistercian monastery may now be mostly in ruins but it is an evocative place, filled in summer with the scent of the many wild flowers which grow in splendid freedom in and around the crumbling grey stones. The abbey was founded in 1156 and eventually owned much of Wensleydale. Sheep, cattle and horses were bred by the monks, who were also the first to make the famous Wensleydale cheese.

Though the buildings are in ruins there is still plenty to see, such as the remains of the staircase known as the Night Stairs, which led the monks down from their upstairs dormitory to night services in the church. Other remains which can be identified include the cloister, the infirmary, the kitchen and the parlour, the only room where talking was permitted – and then only when absolutely necessary. The abbey was destroyed with particular ferocity when Henry VIII began his Dissolution of the Monasteries in 1536. The last Abbot of Jervaulx, Adam Sedbar (or Sedburgh), was a vociferous opponent of the Dissolution and his protests caused him to be hanged at Tyburn Hill.

Jervaulx is on private land but open access is allowed to visitors, with an honesty box for admission money, and there is a car park with a tearoom and shop opposite the entrance.

LEYBURN North Yorkshire Map ref SE1190

Leyburn is yet another of the towns that has, over the years, staked a claim to being the unofficial capital of Wensleydale. It flourished when plague badly affected the village of Wensley in 1563, though the all-important

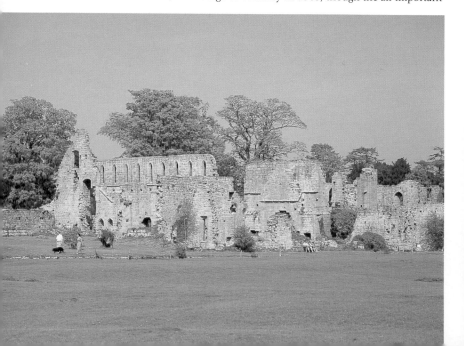

market charter was granted to Askrigg and Leyburn did not receive its own charter until 1684. The Friday market still survives, in and around the large market square. A modern addition is a purpose-built auction centre on Harmby Road, the largest outside London, which holds general and specialist sales two or three times a month. The sales range from the more mundane bric-à-brac of house clearances to expensive collections of fine antiques, old cars and ceramics.

Close by is a ceramics workshop where you will find the Teapottery, an unusual if not unique establishment which makes and displays nothing but teapots. Visitors can watch the craftspeople at work, making pots in every shape and size – the only thing they do not make are teapots that look like teapots.

There are many other craft shops in Leyburn, scattered among the mainly 19th-century town houses. On the western edge of the town, starting in Shawl Terrace not far from the Tourist Information Centre, is the walk to the area known as the Leyburn Shawl. This easy stroll to an open grassy area is a popular walk for locals and visitors alike, as it leads very quickly to some glorious views of Wensleydale.

MASHAM North Yorkshire Map ref SE2280
Visitors to Masham (pronounced Massam) are welcomed by its huge cobbled Market Place, one of the largest in the country and providing ample car parking right in the centre of the town. It is an indication that Masham was once much more important than it appears today, a pleasant but less bustling town than many, though the visitor is guaranteed a busy day. Masham's position was

The Leyburn Shawl is a pleasant walk offering breath-taking views

THE MASHAM SHEEP FAIR
The origins of this fair go back to 1250, when it was granted by charter. It flourished so successfully that as many as 70,000 sheep would be exhibited and sold, but the show died out after World War I with the spread of road and rail transport, and the ease of taking sheep direct to the larger auctions, rather than drive them along the road to Masham. The event was revived in 1986, however, when a local woman, Susan Cunliffe-Lister, decided that Sheep Aid could be added to events like Live Aid and Fashion Aid as a means of raising money to help alleviate the African famines. The Sheep Fair flourished, and still does, with rare and prize sheep on display, sheepdog demonstrations, crafts and other attractions.

THE CRITICS OF JULIUS
CAESAR

Towards the end of the 19th
century, a painter with the
marvellous name of Julius
Caesar Ibbetson lived in a
house in Masham's Chapman
Lane. His rural landscapes are
on display in many of Britain's
art galleries, but his first critics
were the children of Masham.
He would put his paintings on
display in his window to hear
what comments the children
playing in the street made
about them.

COLSTERDALE

To the west of Masham is one
of the least-known Dales, the
lonely and lovely Colsterdale,
with a road that leads
nowhere except to some
peace and fine views. It is a
fitting place for a memorial to
the Yorkshire regiment known
as the Leeds Pals, who were
massacred in July 1916 during
the Battle of the Somme.

*The spire of St Mary's at
Masham stands tall among
the trees*

its making, between the sheep-filled hills of Wensleydale
and the flatter crop-growing fields of the Vale of York. It
was also within easy reach of both Fountains Abbey to
the south, and Jervaulx Abbey a short distance to the
north. In those days its large Market Place was much
needed, not merely for its weekly market but also its
annual Sheep Fair, both of which date back to 1250 (see
side panel on page 91).

Off one corner of the Market Place stands the parish
church of St Mary, whose strange-looking tower came
about in the 15th century when a bell-stage and a tall
spire were added to the original Norman base. The
church was mentioned in the Domesday Book and its
oldest feature is a carved Anglo-Saxon cross dating back
to the 9th century, with some dispute as to what the
now-weathered carvings first represented.

Noted for its fine craft shops, Masham's heritage also
rests in its brewing industry, with two breweries open for
inspection. The longer established is Theakston's, with a
Visitor Centre and the chance to see some of the
country's few remaining coopers at work, building their
barrels. Full guided tours of the brewery must be booked
in advance. The same applies to the Black Sheep
Brewery, so called because it belongs to a renegade
member of the Theakston family – the full saga of
business comings and goings and buy-outs and sell-outs
would make a fair-sized novel.

MIDDLEHAM   North Yorkshire Map ref SE1287
Middleham's claim to be Yorkshire's smallest town is not
the least of its distinctions, as it can also boast two
market places and a collection of horse-racing stables
that have seen it referred to as the 'Newmarket of the

north'. It has certainly produced its share of winners over the years, and of course the racecourses of Thirsk, Ripon, Wetherby and York are all near by. Anyone staying in Middleham will wake up to the clip-clop of hooves on cobbles as the stable lads and lasses take the horses up to the gallops on the moors above the town for an early-morning workout.

Middleham's main feature is its splendid Norman Castle (English Heritage), which is in a good state of preservation. Some of the present remains date back to 1170, although there was another castle in Middleham prior to that. The castle was put on the map by Richard III, who first came to Middleham in 1461 when he was Duke of Gloucester. His tutor in riding and other skills was the Earl of Warwick, and Richard married his daughter, Anne, in 1472. They stayed at Middleham after marriage – their son, Edward, was born in the castle – and lived here until Richard became king in 1483, when he was required to leave for London. By 1485 he was dead, killed in the Battle of Bosworth Field, and Middleham never resumed its royal importance.

Richard would have attended Middleham's church, St Alkelda's, much of which dates back to the 13th and 14th centuries. From the lower market place are splendid views down the dale, and with no lack of pubs, tea shops, gift shops, accommodation and eating places, Middleham shows that it may be a small town but it has a great deal to offer.

Middleham is a small but distinguished town, and much of it is protected as a conservation area

WENSLEYDALE WILD BOARS

Once common in the Yorkshire Dales, the White Boar was adopted as a rallying banner by Richard III when he was at Middleham Castle in the 1480s. The 'Swine Cross' of 1479 in Middleham's upper market place has an animal carved on it which may be a White Boar. Wild boars became extinct in the 17th century, but a herd is now farmed by Wensleydale Wild Boar Breeders, near Ripon.

Middleham and Jervaulx Abbey

An easy walk by the riverside and through woodland, mostly on marked tracks, with the added historical interest of Middleham Castle and Jervaulx Abbey. This is a good walk for summer or dry autumn days.

Time: 3 hours. Distance: 7½ miles (12km).
Location: Middleham is 2 miles (3.2km) south of
Leyburn on the A6108.
Start: Park in Middleham Market Place. (OS grid ref: SE127877.)
OS Maps: Outdoor Leisure 30 (Yorkshire Dales – Northern &
Central areas) 1:25,000. Explorer 302 Northallerton & Thirsk,
Catterick & Bedale 1:25,000.
See Key to Walks on page 121.

ROUTE DIRECTIONS

From Market Place walk to the sign for **Middleham Castle** and go left into the cobbled alley by the Castle Keep Tea Rooms in Canaan Lane. Walk ahead passing Middleham Castle on your right. Continue through the gate and field. It is in this area that the £2½ million **Middleham Jewel** was found. At the end of the field go through the gate and continue as before, but with the wall now on your left. Walk down to the River Cover.

Turn left over a stile in the fence and walk along the river. This woodland path is easy to follow. Continue along the riverbank. Go through the gate into a field and head to the right of the gate at the far side. Stay by the river to reach the **stepping stones**. Cross the river here, continue up the path, through the gate and turn left along the embankment. The path is clear, with occasional stiles and signposts leading to

Cover Bridge.

Cross the road and pass through a gate marked 'Public Footpath/Private Fishing', and follow the wide embankment. Go through a gate, and another after half a mile (800m). The path continues for another half

mile (800m) until you leave it through another gate, turning right along a track which leads to a road. Turn left on to the road and continue until you reach the entrance to **Jervaulx Abbey** (open access) on your left.

After visiting the abbey retrace your steps to Cover Bridge and the **Coverbridge Inn**. Cross the bridge and turn left past the pub and the bungalow. Here a narrow gap in the wall leads you back to the River Cover, where you turn right to skirt the pasture. Go through a gate and follow the path along the riverbank. The path is now well-walked, and after several hundred yards watch for a stile in the wall on your right, which leads to another wall with a stile and two yellow arrows above it (beyond this wall are the stepping stones you crossed earlier).

Don't cross this stile but turn right up the field, and

out through a gate. This leads into Straight Lane, a path which becomes a wider track. Some way beyond a house on your right, turn left through a tiny gap in the wall. Go up the field, turning left when you reach the wall at the far end and skirt round to a small stile to your right. Climb this and cross the field to another stile which takes you down a delightful high-hedged path to rejoin Canaan Lane.

POINTS OF INTEREST

Middleham Castle
This was a favourite place of Richard III, who trained here as a knight. Edward IV and Henry VI were both imprisoned in Middleham during the Wars of the Roses. The central keep, one of the largest in England, dates back to the 12th century.

Middleham Jewel
This magnificent gold and sapphire pendant of the late 15th century was found in 1985. It reached £2½ million at auction, when funds were raised to keep it in Britain. The original is now in the Yorkshire Museum in York, with a replica at Middleham Castle.

using concrete stones, but workmen found these ancient stones buried in the river bed and replaced them.

Jervaulx Abbey
Founded in 1156 by Savigny monks who later became Cistercians, Jervaulx is known as the original home of Wensleydale cheese, and for the breeding of

Daisies grow amid the old stones at Jervaulx Abbey

racehorses, continued today in Middleham.

Coverbridge Inn
Without this inn, with its 16th-century beams, there might be no Wensleydale cheese. Created at Jervaulx Abbey, the recipe for the cheese was passed to the landlord after the dissolution of Jervaulx in 1536. He sold the cheese for 40 years as Coverham cheese, before passing on the recipe which then reverted to the famous name of Wensleydale.

Stepping Stones
The track from Middleham to Jervaulx dates back to the 11th century, and these are believed to be the original stones. They were thought lost until a few years ago when plans were made to reinstate the ancient path,

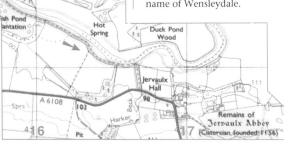

FARFIELD MILL

On the edge of town, down by the River Clough, Fairfield Mill is a restored early Victorian textile mill. As well as Dobcross and Hattersley looms producing fine quality fabrics, there is an art and craft gallery, a textile heritage museum, a pottery, woodworkers, a café, shop and woodland walks. The mill is run by a Trust who are seeking to restore substantial links between farming and industry in rural life.

Sedbergh reveals an appealing mixture of architectural styles

SEDBERGH Cumbria Map ref SD6591

Thanks to the quirks of government boundary changes, the largest town in the Yorkshire Dales National Park is in Cumbria. Even so, Sedbergh's population is still under 3,000 and it has an eye-catching setting. To the north are the high Howgill Fells; to the south the green fields fall away, across the River Rawthey to the River Dee, which runs through Dentdale. Sedbergh is a popular centre, not least because it is only 5 miles (8km) east from junction 37 of the M6 and is the main western gateway to the Dales, it also has a National Park Centre on Main Street. Here you will find interpretative displays and plenty of maps, walks, guides and detailed local information for visitors who intend to stride out and enjoy the beauty of the Yorkshire Dales.

The Normans gave Sedbergh its parish church and a motte and bailey castle. Little remains of the castle save a few grassy mounds and the name of the road leading to it, Castleshaw, but the Church of St Andrew is worth seeing, with its ancient pews and alms boxes. Close by is the minuscule Market Place, where a market has been held for almost 750 years. The Market Cross was

unfortunately removed in 1897 when Finkle Street was widened and other alterations made to the town as part of Queen Victoria's Diamond Jubilee celebrations. The top of the cross now stands in the garden of the Quaker Meeting House in Brigflatts, a tiny village just over a mile (1.6km) southwest of Sedbergh off the Kirkby Lonsdale road. The village was once a small industrial community and the Meeting House, built in 1675, can still be visited. It is the oldest in the north of England, retains many of its original furnishings and has been justly described by many writers as one of the most peaceful places anyone could imagine.

Sedbergh School goes back even further; it was founded in 1525 by a local man, Roger Lupton, who went on to become both Canon of Windsor and Provost of Eton. He founded the school for 'theym of Sedber, Dent, and Garstall', though today it is one of the best-known public schools in the country. A new school was built in 1716, which is now used as a museum and library, and the buildings in use today date mainly from the late 19th century.

It is the old buildings of Sedbergh that are its main attraction. Much of the Main Street has been designated a Conservation Area. As well as narrow alleys and tucked-away yards, Main Street contains many fine dwellings. Webster's Chemist's Shop dates from the first half of the 17th century, and behind it is Weaver's Yard, where the first weaving looms in Sedbergh were set up. From here, at the back of Webster's, a 17th-century chimney breast can be seen – one of the many places around Britain in which Bonnie Prince Charlie is said to have hidden at one time or another. Some of Sedbergh's other delights are hidden, too, so be sure to make time to wander the streets and enjoy this delightful little town.

An air of simple peace surrounds the ancient Friends' Meeting House at Brigflatts

THE PREACHER-BUILDER
The founder of the well-known British construction company, John Laing, lived in Sedbergh for many years; he was responsible in the 1880s for several of the Sedbergh School buildings. Laing was also a preacher at the United Reformed Church which can be found where Main Street meets Joss Lane, opposite the entrance to the National Park Centre car park.

OLD BOYS
Founded in 1525, Sedbergh School is a distinguished public school which includes the son of William Wordsworth as one of its past pupils, as well as the England Rugby Union player, Will Carling. Not so distinguished was Hartley Coleridge, son of the poet, who taught at the school until his dismissal after a heavy bout of drinking!

Semer Water, stretching for half a mile teems with wildfowl in winter

THE SEMER WATER SERVICE

In August 1956 the vicar of nearby Askrigg instituted the first of what has become an annual event: the holding of an open-air service on the shores of Yorkshire's largest natural lake. He was inspired, as he drove past the lake regularly, by the thought of Jesus preaching from a fishing boat. Today the vicar is carried out to a boat just off-shore, and from there preaches to the crowds who come specially for this service, swelling the already large numbers of people enjoying the lake's recreational facilities on the Sunday of the August Bank Holiday weekend.

SEMER WATER North Yorkshire Map ref SD9187

Yorkshire's largest natural lake was formed in Raydale during the Ice Age when a retreating glacier left behind a huge clay dam, and another was blocked in by a glacier in Wensleydale. The resultant melt water formed the lake, which is now a very popular place with anglers, boaters, watersports enthusiasts, nature lovers, hardy swimmers, walkers and those who simply want to admire the splendid views.

It is possible to walk around the lake, which is ringed by three pretty little villages – Countersett, Marsett and Stalling Busk – with a fourth settlement said to be lying on the bed of the lake! Another explanation for the lake's origins claims that a beautiful city once stood here. An angel, disguised as a beggar, went round the city appealing for food and drink, but was turned away at every home. The angel left the city and finally found food and shelter in the home of a poor man and his wife. On leaving the next morning, the angel turned to the city and said:

'Semerwater rise – Semerwater sink,
And cover all save this lile house
that gave me meat and drink.'

The waters did indeed rise to create the lake, and beneath its surface you may just hear the occasional sound of bells ringing from the long-drowned city. The poor man's cottage naturally survived, and is said to be at Low Blean, on the eastern edge of Semer Water.

WENSLEY   North Yorkshire Map ref SE0989

Wensley is one of the small villages that people pass through on their way to the attractions of the dale which gave the village its name. It is hard to imagine that this was once the principal settlement in Wensleydale, being the first place to receive a market charter, as long ago as 1202, and having the only market in the whole of the dale for the following 100 years. Wensley flourished until plague struck the village in 1563, when the focus of Wensleydale life shifted a mile (1.6km) to the east, to Leyburn, and later westward to Askrigg and then Hawes.

The Church of the Holy Trinity remains as a reminder of that former importance, with parts dating from 1240. Its attractive pale stone tower was built in 1719, and it includes an 18th-century pulpit and a 17th-century font. There is also a memorial to members of the Scrope family, from Castle Bolton (see page 83), who had close connections with the church. When the Scropes built Bolton Hall in 1678 Wensley began its regrowth as an estate village.

Near the church is the gate which leads to Bolton Hall, and also near here is the river on which there is a small waterfall and also Wensley Mill. Today this houses the White Rose Candles Workshop, which has been on the site since 1978. Visitors can watch the fascinating process of candle making, and naturally there is a shop.

THE NAME OF THE DALE

Wensleydale is the only major dale not named after the river – the Ure – that runs through it, though it was at one time known as Uredale. This was later supplanted by the name of its then major town, Wensley. In the 12th century, Wensleydale was recorded as Wandelesleydale. The long name means Waendel's woodland clearing in a valley, though it is not known who Waendel was. His woodland clearing was obviously in what we now know as Wensley, and the dale suffix comes from either the Old English word dael, or the Old Scadinavian dalr, both of which mean a valley.

Candle-making is a small but flourishing industry in the village of Wensley

THE BURNING OF BARTLE

A fascinating tradition takes place in the village of West Witton, to the east of West Burton, one evening every August. The origins are unknown, and who Bartle is remains a mystery, although the feast used to take place on St Bartholomew's Day (now the nearest Saturday), to whom the parish church is dedicated. Bartle's straw effigy is carried around the village by two men accompanied by a caller. They visit houses and, of course, pubs, where they are given drinks by the landlord. At each stop the caller sings a long verse, to which all must reply 'Hooray!'. At the end of the evening the effigy is burnt, while everyone sings. During the day there is the village show and races.

West Burton nestling in its rich green valley

WEST BURTON North Yorkshire Map ref SE0186

This beautiful village is just off Wensleydale, at the point where Walden Beck flows out of Waldendale and into Bishopdale, giving West Burton a delightful waterfall, Burton Force, just a short stroll from the village centre. Below the fall is a packhorse bridge, which adds to the charm of the scene.

At West Burton's centre is one of the largest village greens in the country, a great expanse like a grassy lake, its sloping sides lined by old stone cottages with tree-covered hills rising up behind them. Many of the cottages were built for workers in the quarrying and lead-mining industries, whose unpleasant jobs must have been compensated, to some extent, by living in this wonderful setting. The main road, such as it is, bypasses the village centre leaving it as an almost timeless place, where children can play and horses can graze and visitors can feel they have stepped back at least 50 years in time. At the heart of the green is a cross, which adds to the sense of age although it was only put up in 1820 and rebuilt in 1889. It is believed that the cross replaced a more ancient marker, as at one time this was the location for a weekly market which catered for the needs of a much larger population.

On one side of the green is a pub, on the other the Cat Pottery which specialises in life-like ceramic cats. Visitors will find these cats draped around the garden which leads to the workshop.

Wensleydale

Leisure Information

Places of Interest

Shopping

Sports, Activities and the Outdoors

Annual Events and Customs

Checklist

Leisure Information

TOURIST INFORMATION CENTRES

Bedale
Bedale Hall. Tel: 01677 424604.
Hawes
Dales Countryside Museum, Station Yard. Tel: 01969 667450.
Leyburn
4 Central Chambers, Railway Street. Tel: 01969 623069.

NATIONAL PARK CENTRES

Aysgarth
Aysgarth Falls. Tel: 01969 663424.
Hawes
Dales Countryside Museum, Station Road. Tel: 01969 667450. Screens provide a 24-hour information service.
Sedbergh
Main Street.
Tel: 01539 620125.

OTHER INFORMATION

English Heritage
37 Tanner Row, York. Tel: 01904 601901.
www.english-heritage.org.uk
Environment Agency
21 Park Square South, Leeds. Tel: 0113 244 0191.

National Trust
Yorkshire Regional Office: Goddards, 27 Tadcaster Road, Dringhouses, York. Tel: 01904 702021.
www.nationaltrust.org.uk
Parking
There are pay-and-display car parks at most of the National Park Centres. Visitors are encouraged to use them as traffic congestion is a problem in some villages.
RSPB
www.rspb.com
Yorkshire Tourist Board
www.ytb.org.uk
Yorkshire Wildlife Trust
10 Toft Green, York. Tel: 01904 659570. www.yorkshire-wildlife-trust.org.uk

ORDNANCE SURVEY MAPS

Landranger 1:50,000 Sheets 98, 99.
Outdoor Leisure 1:25,000 Sheets 2, 19, 30.

Places of Interest

There will be an admission charge at the following places of interest unless otherwise stated.
Bedale Hall
Bedale. Tel: 01677 424604.

Seventeenth-century mansion with Palladian and Georgian extensions housing local museum and fire engine dated 1742. Open Easter–Sep most days; Tue only in winter.
Black Sheep Brewery Visitor Centre
Masham. Tel: 01765 689227. Traditional working brewery with a visitor centre, shop and bistro. Open all year most days. Guided tours daily; evening tours by arrangement. The tour is not suitable for the infirm. Special events are held throughout the year.
Bolton Castle
Castle Bolton. Tel: 01969 623981. Medieval castle, completed in 1399, overlooking Wensleydale. Tapestries, arms and armour can be seen. Open all year daily.
Crakehall Water Mill
Little Crakehall, Bedale. Tel: 01677 423240. Visitors can buy flour ground at the mill. Open Easter–Sep most days.
Dales Countryside Museum
Station Yard, Hawes. Tel: 01969 667494/667450. Displays include an extensive collection of bygones and farming implements illustrating

Thorpe Perrow Arboretum fills with blossom in springtime

the changing landscape and communities in the area. Full Natinal Park and tourist information service. Open all year. Fee for museum, no charge for entry to National Park Centre.

Jervaulx Abbey
Ruined Cistercian monastery in a beautiful parkland setting, with splendid wild flowers. Open access.

Middleham Castle
Middleham. 2 miles (3.2km) south of Leyburn on A6108. Tel: 01969 623899. The town is dominated by the impressive ruins of 12th-century keep. Childhood home of Richard III. Open Apr–Dec daily; Jan–Mar closed Mon and Tue.

Outhwaite and Son
Town Foot, Hawes. Tel: 01969 667487. Visitors can see rope being made. Open all year weekdays; also Sat Jul–Oct. Free.

Theakston Brewery Visitor Centre
The Brewery, Masham. Tel: 01765 689057. Visitors can watch brewery coopers at work repairing casks. Open most days; telephone for shop opening and tour times.

Thorp Perrow Arboretum
Bedale. Tel: 01677 425323. Open all year daily.

Wensleydale Creamery Visitor Centre
Gayle Lane, Hawes. Tel: 01969 667664. Viewing gallery, museum. Open all year daily.

White Rose Candles
Wensley Mill, Wensley, near Leyburn. Tel: 01969 623544. Watch candles being made. Open Jun–Nov, closed Wed and Sat; Dec open Suns only. Free.

Yorkshire Carriage Museum
Yore Mill, Yorebridge, Aysgarth. (1¾ miles/2.8km east on unclassified road north of A684. Turn right at Palmer Flatt Hotel, museum 300 yards/274m). Tel: 01969 663399. Collection of Victorian horse-drawn

vehicles and handmade scale models of American and English coaches and carriages. Open Easter–Oct daily.

The following places may be of interest to visitors with children. Unless otherwise stated there will be an admission charge.

The Big Sheep and Little Cow Farm
Aiskew Watermill, Aiskew, Bedale. Tel: 01677 422125. Guided tour of farm and animals. Children can feed the lambs; pony rides (additional charge). Open early Apr–Sep daily.

Holme Farm
Sedbergh. Off A683. Tel: 01539 620654. Working farm by river, with nature trails, baby animals. Open Mar–Sep daily.

Shopping

Bedale
Open-air market, Tue.
Hawes
Open-air livestock and street market, Tue.
Leyburn
Open-air livestock and produce market, Fri.
Masham
Open-air market, Wed.
Sedbergh
Open-air market, Wed.

LOCAL SPECIALITIES

Cheese and Honey
Apart from the Wensleydale Creamery in Hawes, many shops stock Wensleydale, Coverdale and other local cheeses, and a very strong-tasting local honey.

Crafts
The Cart House, Hardraw. Tel: 01969 667691. Craft items, gifts, tearoom.
Dent Crafts Centre, Helmside, Dent. Tel: 015396 25400. Crafts, gifts, demonstrations, restaurant, play area. Open Easter–Nov, daily; telephone for winter times.

Glass
Masham Studios: Uredale Glass,

Market Place, Masham.
Tel: 01765 689780. Glass-
blowing demonstrations and
shop.

Ice-cream
Brymor Ice-Cream Parlour near
Jervaulx sells over 30 flavours of
ice-cream, made on the farm
from their own cream.
Open daily. Tel: 01677 460377.

Jewellery
The Rock and Gem Shop, off
Market Place, Hawes. Tel: 01969
667092.
Gemstone jewellery, minerals
and crystals.

Pottery
The Aysgarth Pottery Emporium,
Main Street, Aysgarth.
Tel: 01969 663503.
The Cat Pottery, Moorside
Design, West Burton.
Tel: 01969 663273. Pottery and
small waterfall.
Masham Pottery, Kings Head
Yard, Market Square, Masham.
Tel: 01765 689762.
Pottery and handmade
jewellery.
The Teapottery, Harmby Road,
Leyburn. Tel: 01969 623839.

Prints and Paintings
Wensleydale Framing and Fine
Art Gallery, Leyburn Business
Park, Harmby Road, Leyburn.
Tel: 01969 623488.

Rope
Outhwaite and Son, Town Foot,
Hawes. Tel: 01969 667487.
Visitors can see rope being made
in the workshops.

Wool Products
Wensleydale Longwool
Sheepshop, Cross Lanes Farm,
Gariston, Leyburn.
Tel: 01969 623840.
Handmade clothing and fleeces
for sale.
Sophie's Wild Woollens, The
Shop on the Green, Vicarage
Lane, Dent.
Tel: 015396 25323.
Knitwear and craft items.

Sports, Activities and the Outdoors

ANGLING

Fly
Hawes Blackburn Farm Trout
Fishery, Gayle. Tel: 01969
667524.

Masham Leighton Reservoir,
4 miles (6.4km) southwest of
Masham; day tickets are on sale
in the car park.
Sedbergh Parts of Lune and
Rawthey, also Clune and Dee.
Permits are available from Three
Peaks Ltd, 25 Main Street. Tel:
015396 20446.

Fly and Coarse
River Ure permits are available
from The Coverbridge Inn,
Coverbridge. Tel: 01969
623250.

CAVING

Sedbergh
Introductory caving trips, some
suitable for families. Paul
Ramsden, Sun Lea, Joss Lane.
Tel: 01539 620828.

CYCLE HIRE

Coverdale
Thwaite Arms, Horsehouse.
Tel: 01969 640206.

GOLF COURSES

Bedale
Bedale Golf Club, Leyburn Road.
Tel: 01677 422451.

Leyburn
Akebar Park Golf Club, Akebar
Park, Wensleydale. Tel: 01677
450201.

Masham
Masham Golf Club, Burnholme,
Swinton Road. Tel: 01765
689379.

GUIDED WALKS

Semer Water Nature Reserve,
Jun–Sep.
Tel: 01969 650330.

HORSE-RIDING

Leyburn
Akebar Park.
Tel: 01677 450201.

Masham
Swinton Riding and Trekking
Centre, Home Farm, Swinton.
Tel: 01765 689241.

LONG-DISTANCE FOOTPATHS

The Herriot Way
A 56-mile (90-km) circular route
from Aysgarth through the
Yorkshire Dales National Park
following an itinerary associated
with James Herriot, the Yorkshire

vet and author, whose stories
were adapted for the film and
television series, *All Creatures
Great and Small*.

Annual Events and Customs

Dent
Dent Gala, late August.

Hardraw
Hardraw Brass Band Festival,
contact The Green Dragon,
Hardraw. Tel: 01969 667392.

Hawes
Hawes Gala, late June.

Jervaulx
The Jervaulx Horse Trials, early
June.

Leyburn
Wensleydale Agricultural Show,
Leyburn, late August.

Masham
Masham Steam Engine and Fair
Organ Rally, mid-July.
Masham Sheep Fair, late
September.

Middleham
Open days in racing stables.
Contact Leyburn Tourist
Information Centre for dates.
Middleham Festival, June

Semer Water
Outdoor church service on
Sunday of August Bank Hol
weekend.

West Witton
The West Witton Feast and the
Burning of Bartle takes place on
the Saturday nearest to 24
August.

The checklists give details of just
some of the facilites within the
area covered by this guide.
Further information can be
obtained from Tourist
Information Centres.

Swaledale and the North

Swaledale is one of the grandest of all the dales, its rugged beauty more appealing to some than the prettier and busier Wensleydale. It is a dale of fast-flowing streams and waterfalls, of a string of small villages with harsh-sounding Norse names such as Keld and Muker. At its eastern end stands Richmond, as busy and civilised a market town as you could wish for, with its castle and no less than three museums. At its western end, visitors will feel they have left civilisation far behind as the road climbs and curves through some dramatic scenery towards Mallerstang, the other main northern dale covered by this chapter. Both are dales of tremendous character.

THE FINAL JOURNEY
Muker's church was built in 1580 as a chapel of ease which offered a respite for the coffin-carriers who previously had to make the journey with their burdens down the 'Corpse Way' to Grinton. The Queen's Inn in Muker, which is no longer a public house, was once one of the stops for the carriers. The Inn kept special tankards for the use of the bearers.

THE SWALEDALE VILLAGES North Yorkshire
Swaledale names are mostly short and sharp, from their Norse origins: Muker, Keld, Thwaite, Reeth, Angram. Even the longer ones are spat out with those same short Norse vowels: Gunnerside, Arkengarthdale. Most of the villages are short and sharp too, strung out along the B6270 like occasional knots in a rope, but they welcome the tourist trade and offer places to stay and eat and a range of local craft studios. Beyond Keld, the 'knots' end, and the lonely road crosses the fells to Nateby and Kirkby Stephen at the northern end of the valley of Mallerstang as it opens out into the Vale of Eden.

Travelling from Reeth, Gunnerside is the first sizeable community. It is an appealing spot with stone cottages, once the homes of lead miners, looking down on the River Swale with high-rising moors as a backdrop. Norse

Muker is an attractive Dales village with few pretensions

settlers were attracted by its sheltered location
at the confluence of Gunnerside Gill and the larger
river. Later lead mining brought prosperity to the area,
and the ruins of several mines can be found just a short
distance from the centre of the village. Another
enjoyable walk from here is to the unusual Ivelet Bridge
(see Walk on page 112).

Beyond Ivelet is Muker, another welcoming collection
of stone cottages clustered in jigsaw streets which zigzag
steeply up from the main road. Plaques on the wall of
the church commemorate Richard (1862–1928) and
Cherry (1871–1940) Kearton, two brothers who were
born in Thwaite and went to school in Muker. They
devoted their lives to watching wildlife and became
early pioneers of wildlife photography. There is also a
Literary Institute, an echo of the Norse origins of its
unusual name, for Muker means 'a cultivated plot'.

Scarcely a mile (1.6km) west of Muker is Thwaite,
where the cottage in which the Kearton brothers were
born still stands. This idyllic place hides the tragedy of
the fearsome flood of 1899 when the waters of Thwaite
Beck swept down from Stock Dale in the west and
almost wiped out the entire community. It is said that
flowers washed from Thwaite's cottage gardens were
later found growing in Muker.

The last Swaledale village is Keld, quietly going about
its business, set back from the main road in a dead end
that leads down to the River Swale and some of
Swaledale's most impressive falls (see Walk on page
108). The Pennine Way passes the edge of Keld before
heading north up Stonesdale to the lonely outpost that
is Tan Hill. The Swaledale road goes west through some
of the most dramatic scenery in the whole of the Dales
before arriving at Nateby just outside the boundary of
the National Park, in the valley of Mallerstang.

Clustered around the beck,
Thwaite lies at the foot of
Kisdon Hill

NORSE NAMES
The Norse word for a
woodland clearing was
'thwaite' or 'thveit', and other
common Norse endings are
'sett' and 'side', which tend to
occur in the north of the
Dales: Appersett, Gunnerside,
Swinithwaite. The 'sett'
ending derives from *saetr*,
which describes the Norse
practice of driving their
animals to the higher pastures
for summer grazing. The
typical isolated Dales barn is
another result of this way of
living. Norse words include
many that are still used today,
such as fell, beck, gill and
force.

To Hellgill and Back

A stirring but not difficult walk over the fells of Mallerstang, taking in little-known waterfalls and superb views of Wild Boar Fell. A spring or summer walk, ideal under fine blue skies.

Time: 1½ hours. Distance: 3 miles (4.8km).
Location: 8 miles (12.8km) south of Kirkby Stephen.
Start: The cluster of houses and farm buildings known as Shaw Paddock has no placename on the road. It is situated on the B6259 Garsdale to Kirkby Stephen road where it swings left under the railway bridge carrying the Settle–Carlisle line. Park with care by the roadside on the wide grass verges.
(OS grid ref: SD785952.)
OS Map: Outdoor Leisure 19
(Howgill Fells & Upper Eden Valley)
1:25,000.
See Key to Walks on page 121.

ROUTE DIRECTIONS

At the point where the road bears left before passing under the bridge, a track begins between two farm buildings leading straight ahead. Go through the gates and keep on the track which winds up the hill ahead. On the left is a superb view of **Wild Boar Fell**. Cross an old stone bridge over the River Ure, ignore the farm entrance to the right, and go straight ahead where the track becomes grassy. Beyond here the track forks; take the left branch, but bear in mind that this is grass-covered and used by vehicles so impressions on the ground can alter. The first stretch is slightly overgrown, but it soon clears to grass again. Head towards three trees whose tops peer over the horizon. Cross the River Ure again on a small stone bridge – the river is almost narrow enough to leap over at this point. The track now heads clearly up to **Hell Gill Bridge** which is visible among the trees.

When you have finished peering over the bridge into the chasm, pass through the gate on the far side, and another gate immediately to the left. This track leads you down past **Hellgill House**. Pass through the farmyard and out through the gate. Continue down the track, but where it turns sharply left, you should hear the sound of a waterfall. Walk across to the right to see **Hellgill Force**.

Continue downwards and pass through a gate which leads you across a railway bridge. Almost immediately opposite is a signposted gateway, beyond which you turn left to pick up a footpath that heads back towards Shaw Paddock. There is a fence on your left, then a wall, and you should aim for a gate in the wall ahead of you. The track is then clearly defined through some reed beds, and ascends. Pass through a gate in the wall on your left; the path now descends. Pass through another gate and turn right on to the B6259. The route continues on the road for a short distance returning to Shaw Paddock.

POINTS OF INTEREST

Wild Boar Fell
The evocative name comes about because the last wild boar in England was said to have been killed here in the 15th century by Sir Richard Musgrave. He was buried in the churchyard at Kirkby Stephen, at the far end of Mallerstang, and when his grave was opened in 1847 while the side chapels were being restored, a boar's tusk was found buried with him. The fell rises to 2,324 feet (708m), from which point it is possible to see the Lake District to the west and the Three Peaks of the Yorkshire Dales to the south.

Hell Gill Bridge
Hell Gill Bridge is also known as Devil's Bridge. According to legend it was at this spot, before the bridge was rebuilt, that Dick Turpin escaped from his pursuers by leaping across the chasm on his horse, Black Bess, thereby showing a clean pair of heels to the law. Other stories, no doubt dictated by local pride, say that the leap was made by Ned Ward, a highwayman who lived at Farclose House, slightly further up the valley of Mallerstang.

Hellgill House
This former inn, known as The Checkers, was a stopping point on the old drovers' road. The old road ran through the dale and was the route taken by men driving their herds of cattle or flocks of geese to market.

Hellgill Force

This is one of the biggest waterfalls in the area, the more impressive for being so well-hidden, particularly when approached from this direction. The strength of the fall depends on the weather but because it is near the source of the river it rises quickly after rain.

Hell Gill is the name given to the cutting and the river which runs through it. This small flow of water serves as a boundary for the parish of Mallerstang. To the north is Cumbria, which was once Westmorland, to the south is North Yorkshire, formerly the North Riding.

The scale of the waterfall at Hellgill is a swift indication of local weather conditions

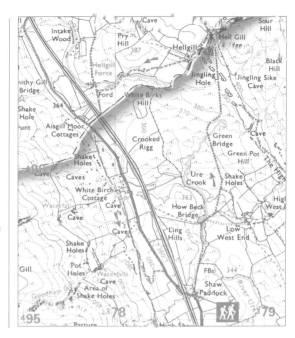

The Keld Waterfalls

A varied walk, best in autumn, along riverside and farm tracks. Mostly easy going with a scramble down to the highlight of the walk – Kisdon Force.

Time: 1½ hours. Distance: 3½ miles (5.6km).
Location: 7 miles (11.2km) north of Hawes on the B6270.
Start: Park in the yard at Park Lodge in Keld (small charge), or in the village. (OS grid ref: NY893012.)
OS Maps: Landranger 92 (Barnard Castle) 1:50,000.
Outdoor Leisure 30 (Yorkshire Dales – Northern & Central areas) 1:25,000.
See Key to Walks on page 121.

ROUTE DIRECTIONS

Take the short path at the far right of the farmer's yard to view **Catrake Force**. Return through the yard, cross the small square in the centre of **Keld** and follow the signpost 'Footpath to Muker', passing the graveyard up to your right. A little further on the Pennine Way is signed to the left and right, take the right-hand path. You can see East Gill Force on your left.

Keep on the path, go through a gate and continue to the sign which directs you left to Upper **Kisdon Force**. The upper falls are quite small, but this is more than compensated for by their beautiful setting, just where the river widens into a pool by limestone cliffs. The path continues down another 20 yards (18m) or so to the lower falls. This is a bit of a scramble but well worth the effort to be able to stand close (but not too close!) to the water's powerful force, washed by its spray, with views back to the upper falls.

Make your way back past the upper falls to the track, and turn right to return to the Pennine Way footpath sign. Turn right again down to the river. Cross the bridge, turn left and follow the path upwards with East Gill Force on your right. Above the waterfall, turn left and walk up to the farmhouse. Turn left, in the farmyard, leaving the Pennine Way which continues up to the right. On the far side of the house, go through a gate to join the farm access road. Catrake Force can be heard, though barely seen, down to the left.

Continue on this clearly-defined road and after half a mile (800m) cross West Stonesdale Beck near the small Currack Force falls. Go through two gates to emerge on the road to West Stonesdale. Here you can turn left down the zigzag Stonesdale Lane to the bridge across the river to enjoy the view. (If you want to shorten the walk here you can cross the bridge and turn left on to the road to return to Keld, turning left into the village just before the youth hostel.) To complete the full walk turn right on Stonesdale Lane and take the first path, immediately on your left, through a gate. Follow the path above the river, passing **Wain Wath Force**. Go over a couple of stiles to a stoney

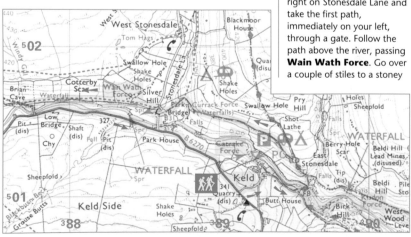

The River Swale spills over the ledges at Wain Wath Falls

path down to the bridge. Cross the bridge, turn left on to the road (usually quiet) to return to Keld.

POINTS OF INTEREST

Catrake Force
The falls are situated on private land, but a good view can be had from the path which leads from the parking area at the farm. On the near side of the falls is the entrance to an old lead mine, which was intended to run 3 miles (4.8km) up river to the source of the Swale, but the lead quickly ran out and the plan never materialised.

Keld
Keld is the last settlement in Swaledale – or the first, depending on which direction you are travelling. Hidden away off the B6270 amid rich, green hills, it has a chapel, farms and old houses built from local stone. There are toilets, a youth hstel, a campsite and a small shop. It is, however, very popular as it is surrounded by several delightful waterfalls and is where the Pennine Way crosses the Coast-to-Coast footpath.

Kisdon Force
The name Kisdon is Celtic, an amalgamation of kis (little), and dun (a detached hill). The hill (not so little at 1,636 feet, 499m) is south of the river. It lends its name to these falls in one of the most pleasing settings in the Dales, hemmed as they are by limestone cliffs. The river once flowed to the west of Kisdon Hill, but a glacial dam near Thwaite diverted the course and gouged out these stunning falls from the limestone terrain.

Wain Wath Force
Cotterby Scar is an impressive backdrop to these falls. On the other side of the road are the remains of the Keldside Lead Smelting Mill, its flue still traceable up the fell to the the stump of a chimney.

Kirkby Stephen was once a coaching town

LOCAL TRADITIONS

A charming tradition kept by parishioners of the Church of St Mary in Outhgill, Mallerstang's only church, is Boon Day. It is held on the first convenient day after the end of hay-making, when they cut the grass in the graveyard and tend the graves – work neglected through the busy hay-making season.

St Mary's shares an unusual feature with the parish church in Kirkby Stephen – both have 18th-century bread shelves. The parish council in Outhgill still administers a charity whereby bread is provided for anyone in the parish over retirement age.

KIRKBY STEPHEN   Cumbria Map ref NY7708

If this unspoilt town started to market itself as yet another 'Gateway to the Dales', no one could complain at the description for although it is in Cumbria, it stands at the foot of Mallerstang, which stretches south, half-in and half-out of the Yorkshire Dales National Park. While Kirkby Stephen tends to get lost between the Yorkshire Dales and the Lake District, the inhabitants know exactly where they stand, referring to their parish church as the 'Cathedral of the Dales', an apt description for a magnificent church.

While the rest of Kirkby Stephen may not quite live up to its impressive parish church, it is still an enjoyable place to linger, with several guesthouses and welcoming pubs, though fewer souvenir shops than you might expect. Many people might think that this is all to the good. The town does attract a large number of visitors as it is on the famous Wainwright Coast-to-Coast walk.

The Church of St Stephen is one of the region's hidden gems, containing many fine features. There are some well-preserved bread shelves, a fine Shap granite and Italian marble pulpit, and a 17th-century font. A beautiful engraved panel over the entrance to the Hartley Chapel shows the Stoning of St Stephen; it was made by John Hutton, who was also responsible for the memorable glass screen in Coventry Cathedral. Inside the Chapel is a tub once used to measure a bushel of wheat. The remains of a 13th-century piscina, a basin with a drain where water used in ceremonial occasions is poured away, can also be seen.

The finest of all the church's features is the Loki Stone, a 10th-century Anglo-Danish cross shaft carved with the features of the Norse God, Loki. The stone is the only such example in Britain, and one of only two in the whole of Europe. The oldest part of the present church dates from 1220. Prior to that, this was the site of a Norman church which only survived for 50 years, and before that a Saxon church is known to have stood here. Exploring the churchyard reveals a flat stone table. This is the Trupp Stone, on which tenants of church properties would traditionally pay their tithes. It was in use until 1836. Also of historical interest are the attractive cloisters at the entrance to the church grounds, where once the Butter Market took place. In sunlight the stone is an appealing buttery colour.

About 4 miles (6,4km) south of Kirkby Stephen, by the side of the B6259, stand the atmospheric remains of Pendragon Castle. In truth there is more atmosphere there than historical fact, for although the castle is named after King Uther Pendragon, the legendary father of King Arthur, the building dates only from the 12th century. It is crumbling and tiny, and although on private land there is open access for the public.

THE CUMBRIA CYCLE WAY
This 259-mile (414-km) route circles Cumbria, mainly on minor roads with some stretches on bridleways and former railway lines. One section of the waymarked route goes through Kirkby Lonsdale, Sedbergh and Garsdale before turning north along Mallerstang to Kirkby Stephen and on through Appleby towards Carlisle. Cyclists wishing to explore this Cumbrian corner of the Yorkshire Dales could take the Settle–Carlisle line to Garsdale Head station and follow the route from there to the next station at Kirkby Stephen. An information leaflet is available from Tourist Information Centres.

The town's parish church is particularly fine

From Gunnerside to Ivelet Bridge

A very easy but enjoyable walk, along the River Swale, to the old haunted bridge at Ivelet. A good autumn walk.

Time: 1½ hours. Distance: 3 miles (4.8km).
Location: On B6270 at Gunnerside.
Start: There is plenty of on-road parking in the centre of Gunnerside, adjacent to the post office.
(OS grid ref: SD951983.)
OS Map: Outdoor Leisure 30
(Yorkshire Dales – Northern & Central areas)
1:25,000.
See Key to Walks on page 121.

ROUTE DIRECTIONS

From the parking area in **Gunnerside**, opposite the King's Head, walk a short distance along the main road in the direction of Muker to the bridge across the River Swale. Just before the bridge is a footpath to the right signed 'Riverside Path'. Take this path down to the banks of the Swale. Watch for **dippers** in the river here. The path is well defined and takes you over a few stiles, through a gap in a wall and over a wooden stile which enables you to continue walking ahead alongside the river.

Go over a wooden stile at the end of the riverside path and take the footpath signed 'Gunnerside'. Follow this path up the hill for a short distance and at the top of the slope turn left and take the footpath signed 'Ivelet'. The path runs alongside a fence on your left, then goes through a gate which puts the fence on your right. The path is well trodden through the pastures, but do heed the signs and keep to single file to prevent destroying too much of the meadowland grazing for the Swaledale sheep. Pass through several more gaps in

the stone walls – some of them very narrow – until you reach the tiny community of Ivelet. In Ivelet, turn left and left again along the road out of the village down to the river and **Ivelet Bridge**. Note the stone on the left on the nearside of the bridge which marks its presence on the **Corpse Way**.

Return along the road, turn left in Ivelet and take the steep climb on a minor road above the village. Cross a cattle grid and go over the brow of the hill bearing right to another old bridge. The road takes you high above the river with excellent views of the Swale valley to both the east and west. This quiet, single-track road from Gunnerside to Ivelet serves the scattering of farms alongside it. You are unlikely to meet very much traffic as it leads you high above the River Swale back to Gunnerside, emerging by the post office.

POINTS OF INTEREST

Gunnerside
Like many of the Swaledale villages, this is an old Norse settlement. Its name was originally Gunnars Seatre, or the Pasture of Gunnar, with Gunnar possibly being the name of the Norse chief who settled there. Gunnerside became one of Swaledale's leading lead-

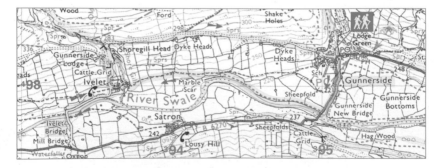

mining centres; its defunct Old Gang Mines are mainly on the uplands above the village. The word 'gang' does not refer to a group of workers, but derives from the Old English word meaning a road, indicating the presence of mines here before the 6th century AD.

Dippers

These dark brown birds with white bibs, like waiters, favour fast-flowing water with rocks on which they perform their unique bobbing/dipping

Gunnerside owes its origins to lead-mining

movement. They are able to go underwater in search of food for short periods of time, running along the river bed.

Ivelet Bridge

Built in 1698, this is one of the finest examples of a packhorse bridge in the Dales, with a severe humpback which makes it impossible for low-slung vehicles to cross. The lane by the bridge is believed to be haunted by a headless black dog, said to have been seen going on to the bridge and disappearing over the side. The locals regard its appearance as an ill omen.

The Corpse Way

The path along the river between Ivelet and Gunnerside is part of the 'Corpse Way'. Bodies were carried for burial at the nearest church, which until 1580 was in Grinton, beyond Reeth. In 1580 the church at Muker was built, shortening the journey. The corpses were carried in wicker baskets and there were traditional resting points along the way. The stone by Ivelet Bridge is one example of this, where the pall bearers could rest their load. Another such halt was at the 17th-century Punch Bowl Inn at Feetham.

THE 'CORPSE WAY' TO GRINTON

The parish church of St Andrew in Grinton was for centuries the church for the whole of Swaledale. People who died in the upper reaches of the Dale would have to be brought to Grinton on what became known as the 'Corpse Way'. There are some Norman remains at the church, although most of it dates from the 13th to 15th centuries. Note the hole in the wall known as the Leper's Squint, which allowed afflicted people to observe the service at a safe distance from the rest of the congregation.

On Reeth's village green the Black Bull rubs shoulders with the King's Arms

REETH North Yorkshire Map ref SE0399

Tucked in the junction where Arkengarthdale meets Swaledale, Reeth appears much larger and more important than the other Swaledale villages. This is due to the huge green which dominates the place, and the sprawling nature of the village itself. Today it is an attractive centre for tourism, with general shops, craft shops, pubs, a few hotels and guesthouses, and the dale's main museum.

The Swaledale Folk Museum, which also acts as an information centre for visitors, is hidden away behind the post office on the far eastern side of the Green. Inside there are particularly good displays on the dale's main industries over the years: farming and lead-mining. The latter is long-gone, and there was some money to be made from the former, as information about a local farmer's sale of a ram for £30,000 indicates.

Reeth received its market charter in 1695, and although there is still a market on Fridays, it is a small affair compared to most places. Of more interest to visitors these days are the several craft shops that are supported by Reeth's main business today: tourism.

About 3 miles (4.8km) west of Reeth, on the minor road which goes north from Feetham, is Surrender Bridge. Just over the bridge on the right is a track which takes you to the remains of the Surrender Lead Smelting Mill, now a scheduled Ancient Monument. There were several lead workings in this area, the industry dates from Roman times but it was at its peak in the 17th and 18th centuries.

RICHMOND North Yorkshire Map ref NZ1701

To approach Richmond from Swaledale is to see the importance of the town to the dale. The road winds through wooded valleys, eventually revealing Richmond Castle standing on its hill high above the river. The castle, now managed by English Heritage, is Norman and inside it Scolland's Hall, from the late 11th century, claims to be the oldest hall in England. The views down over the river are splendid.

Behind the castle is Richmond's huge cobbled Market Place, with its Market Cross and the unusual sight of Holy Trinity Church: unusual because there are shops and a museum built into the base of the building, which was almost destroyed several times, then restored, since its first construction in around 1150. The curfew bell which sounds automatically every day from the church's clocktower, at 8am and 8pm, is also known as the 'Prentice Bell. This is because as well as sounding the curfew, it marked the start and end of the apprentices' working day. Responsibility for ringing it lay with the Town Crier, whose house was at the foot of the bell tower. A convenient rope meant that the morning bell could be rung without him having to get out of bed.

Richmond's church shares the cobbled square with a curious obelisk, raised in 1771

BEATING THE BOUNDARY

The custom of beating or marking the boundaries of Richmond is incorporated into the Royal Charter of 1576, but it is believed to be a much older tradition. It was intended to avoid disputes over the exact boundaries with neighbouring estates and boroughs, so here it is a civic matter rather than a religious custom as happens in other parishes. In Richmond the 14-mile (22-km) walk takes place every seven years in August and ends with races and games for children.

POOR OLD HORSE

The 'Poor Old Horse' is a mummer's play performed in and around Richmond in the week before Christmas and up to New Year's Eve. During the play the horse dies, but rises again in a reflection of its traditional pagan role as a bringer of good luck and fertility. Poor Old Horse is accompanied by red-coated attendants, redolent of the Richmond Hunt, and can traditionally be found in the town centre on Christmas Eve.

SWEET LASS OF RICHMOND HILL

Though often claimed by Richmond upon Thames, the Sweet Lass of Richmond Hill was Frances I'Anson, who lived at Hill House, Pottergate. She married a barrister, Leonard McNalley, in 1787, who was inspired to write the words of 'Sweet Lass of Richmond Hill', which was set to music by James Hook. Sadly Frances died at the age of 29.

The castle's square keep is a proud landmark above the town

The museum in the church is that of the Green Howards, one of Yorkshire's proudest regiments. Inside are smart modern displays, which the historian or military buff will find fascinating, but this is only one of three museums that Richmond can boast. The Richmondshire Museum itself is a typical miscellaneous collection of historical items, ancient and modern, from the prehistoric to the television age of James Herriot. When the BBC finished filming the first series of *All Creatures Great and Small*, not knowing that when screened it would go on to become one of the most popular series ever made, they sold the set for James Herriot's surgery to the museum. With a second series on the horizon, the BBC asked if they could buy it back, but the museum, sensing by then that it had an exhibit of great interest to visitors, refused. The BBC was forced to build a replacement. No doubt James Herriot would have recognised the canny Yorkshire business dealings.

Richmond's best museum, however, is the Georgian Theatre Museum – a living museum if ever there was one. This Georgian Theatre was built in 1788, the only one in the world that still survives in its original state. As well as attending a show in the evenings, visitors should take one of the guided tours to have a glimpse behind (and below) the stage, into the dressing rooms and inside the original box office. The enthusiastic volunteer guides really make the place come alive.

About a mile (1.6km) to the southeast of the town centre, accessible via a walk along the banks of the River Swale, is Easby Abbey in the care of English Heritage. The ruins of this medieval monastery are impressive, if not quite as grand as the more celebrated Fountains Abbey further south. They certainly make a fitting destination for a pleasant walk, though, where Swaledale comes to an end.

TAN HILL North Yorkshire Map ref NY8907

The lonely Tan Hill Inn is the highest pub in England at 1,732 feet (528m), reached via a hairpin road from Keld, 4 miles (6.4km) to the south. It makes the hamlet of Keld look like a city's bright lights. Tan Hill is right on the County Durham boundary – in fact boundary changes in 1974 moved the inn from Yorkshire into Durham, but after loyal Yorkshiremen objected to losing their celebrated pub, the boundary was redrawn to the north.

There is no public transport to the pub, so if you wish to visit this isolated spot it will have to be on foot or by car, and preferably during opening hours. It once had its own working coal mine, and was a gathering point for the farmers and miners who worked in this area. 'Tan' is the Celtic word for a fire, so the first flames on this hill may go back to the Beltane fires of the Celts on May Day, and Walpurgis Night, the eve of Beltane.

The pub became established because it is at a junction of roads, with Arkengarthdale to the east and the switchback road towards Brough in Cumbria to the west, both long used by pedlars on their way to the Yorkshire markets. Children born at Tan Hill in the early 20th century had to walk to school in Keld, with the harder (uphill) task of walking home again at the end of the day. In bad weather conditions they would be found lodgings in Keld during the week.

The pub that's on top of the world

TAN HILL TRIALS

In their authoritative book, *Swaledale*, first published in 1934, Ella Pontefract and Marie Hartley tell how hound trials were once common at Tan Hill, in the days when mines were in production and Stonesdale was slightly more populous. Bare-knuckle boxing bouts were also popular, and one memorable encounter was when a local man, George Kearton of Oxnop Hall near Muker, took on the Westmorland champion and won. After washing off the sweat and blood in the same tub, the two men drank together for a week to show there were no hard feelings. George Kearton died in 1764 at the grand old age of 124.

Swaledale and The North

Checklist

- Leisure Information
- Places of Interest
- Shopping
- The Performing Arts
- Sports, Activities and the Outdoors
- Annual Events and Customs

Leisure Information

TOURIST INFORMATION CENTRES

Richmond
Friary Gardens, Victoria Road.
Tel: 01748 850252/825994.

OTHER INFORMATION

British Waterways Board Headquarters
Willow Grange, Church Road, Watford. Tel: 01923 226422.
www.british-waterways.org
English Heritage
37 Tanner Row, York. Tel: 01904 601901.
www.english-heritage.org.uk
Environment Agency
21 Park Square South, Leeds.
Tel: 0113 244 0191.
National Trust
Yorkshire Regional Office

James Herriot's surgery in Richmondshire Museum, Richmond

Goddards, 27 Tadcaster Road, Dringhouses, York.
Tel: 01904 702021.
www.nationaltrust.org.uk
Parking
Pay-and-display parking is available throughout the district with limited free disc parking in Richmond. The parking discs can normally be obtained at Tourist Information Centres, shops, banks etc.
Yorkshire Wildlife Trust
10 Toft Green, York. Tel: 01904 659570. www.yorkshire-wildlife-trust.org.uk

ORDNANCE SURVEY MAPS

Landranger 1:50,000 Sheets 92, 98.
Outdoor Leisure 1:25,000 Sheet 30.

Places of Interest

There will be an admission charge at the following places of interest unless otherwise stated.

Easby Abbey
Richmond. Impressive medieval abbey remains (English Heritage) set beside the River Swale. Open site, access any reasonable time. Free.
Georgian Theatre Royal
Victoria Road, Richmond.
Tel: 01748 823710.
Dating from 1788, the theatre closed down in 1848, but was restored and re-opened in 1962. The theatre is still used for live productions and it has a museum with old playbills, photographs and the oldest complete set of painted scenery in the country.
Open Apr–Oct, daily.
Green Howards Regimental Museum
Trinity Church Square, Market Place, Richmond.
Tel: 01748 822133.
The history of the Green Howards, going back to the 17th century, is illustrated here, together with displays of uniforms, weapons and medals.
Open Feb, Mar & Nov, weekdays; Apr–Oct Mon–Sat.
Richmond Castle
Richmond.
Tel: 01748 822493.
Occupying a stunning position overlooking the River Swale, the castle is now in ruins, but visitors can see the keep, two of the towers and Scolland's Hall.
Open Apr–Oct daily; Nov–Mar most days except Christmas and New Year's Day.
Richmondshire Museum
Ryder's Wynd, Richmond.
Tel: 01748 825611.

Museum of local history.
Open Easter–Oct, daily.
Swaledale Folk Museum
off the Green, Reeth.
Tel: 01748 884373. Illustrates
the history of the area.
Open Easter–Oct, daily.

SPECIAL INTEREST FOR CHILDREN

The following places may be of
interest to visitors with children.
Unless otherwise stated there
will be an admission charge.
Georgian Theatre Royal
Victoria Road, Richmond. Tel:
01748 823710. Dating back to
1780, the theatre closed down
in 1848, but was then restored
and re-opened in 1962. The
theatre is still used for live
productions and it has a
museum with old playbills,
photographs and the oldest
completed set of painted
scenery in the country. Open
Apr–Oct daily.
**Green Howards Regimental
Museum**
Trinity Church Square,
Richmond. Tel: 01748 822133.
The history of the Green
Howards going back to the 17th
century is illustrated here
together with displays of
uniforms, weapons and medals.
Open Feb, Mar & Nov,
weekdays; Apr–Oct Mon–Sat.
Richmond Castle
Richmond. Tel: 01748 822493.
Occupying a stunning position
overlooking the River Swale.
Although the castle is now in
ruins, you can see the keep, two
of the towers and the Scolland's
Hall. Open Apr–Oct daily;
Nov–Mar most days except
Christmas and New Year's Day.
Richmondshire Museum
Ryder's Wynd, Richmond.
Tel: 01748 825611. Museum of
local history. Open Easter–Oct
daily.

Shopping

Kirkby Stephen
There are antiques shops in
Market Street. Open-air market,
Mon.
Reeth
Open-air market, Fri.

Richmond
Open-air market Sat. Indoor
market Tue, Thu, Fri & Sat.

LOCAL SPECIALITIES

Craft workshop
Reeth Dales Centre, Silver Street,
Reeth. A collection of craft
workshops including Philip
Bastow, cabinet maker.
Tel: 01748 884555.
Outdoor Equipment
P N Denby, Market Square,
Kirkby Stephen.
Tel: 017683 71671.
Pottery
Garden House Pottery, The
Smithy, Anvil Square, Reeth.
Tel: 01748 884188.
Sculptures and Portraits
Joy Bentley, East Windy Hall,
Arkengarthdale Road, Reeth.
Tel: 01748 884316.
Steff's, Reeth Dales Centre, Silver
Street, Reeth. Tel: 01748
884498. Animal sculptures and
models, hand-painted.
Wall and Mantel Clocks
Clockworks, Reeth Dales Centre,
Silver Street, Reeth.
Tel: 01748 884088.
Woollens
Swaledale Woollens, Strawbeck,
Muker. Tel: 01748 886251.

The Performing Arts

Georgian Theatre Royal
Victoria Road, Richmond.
Tel: 01748 823710/823021

Sports, Activities and the Outdoors

ANGLING

Fly and Coarse
River Swale Richmond and
District Angling Society have 14
miles (22.4km) of fishing rights;
permits are avaialble from
Richmond Angling Centre.
Tel: 01748 822989.
Also from Gilsan Sports shop in
Richmond.
Tel: 01748 822108.

CYCLE HIRE

Richmond
Arthur Caygill Cycles,
Gallowfields Trading Estate.
Tel: 01748 825469.

GOLF COURSES

Richmond
The Richmond (Yorkshire) Golf
Club, Bend Hagg.
Tel: 01748 823231.

GUIDED WALKS

For information about guided
walks in the area, contact the
local Tourist Information
Centres.

HELICOPTER FLIGHTS

Pennine Helicopters Ltd,
Oakdene Farm, Stanedge,
Saddleworth, Greater
Manchester.
Tel: 01457 820152.
Flights over the Yorkshire Dales.

HORSE-RIDING

Richmond
Brookleigh Riding Centre,
Forcett.
Tel: 01325 718286.

Annual Events and Customs

Muker
Muker Show, early September.
Reeth
Reeth Show, late August.
Richmond
The Richmond Meet, Spring
Bank Hol weekend.
The 'Poor Old Horse' Mummers'
Play takes place around
Christmas.
Swaledale
The Swaledale Festival, late May
to early June.

The checklists give details of just
some of the facilities within the
area covered by this guide.
Further information can be
obtained from Tourist
Information Centres.

Atlas and Map Symbols

THE NATIONAL GRID SYSTEM

The National Grid system covers Great Britain with an imaginary network of 100 kilometre grid squares. Each square is given a unique alphabetic reference as shown in the diagram. These squares are sub-divided into one hundred 10 kilometre squares, each numbered from 0 to 9 in an easterly (left to right) direction and northerly (upwards) direction from the bottom left corner. Each 10 km square is similarly sub-divided into one hundred 1 km squares.

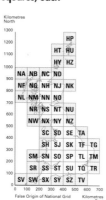

Kilometres North

			HP
	HT	HU	
	HY	HZ	
NA	NB	NC	ND
NF	NG	NH	NJ NK
NL	NM	NN	NO
NR	NS	NT	NU
NW	NX	NY	NZ
	SC	SD	SE TA
	SH	SJ	SK TF TG
	SM	SN	SO SP TL TM
	SR	SS	ST SU TQ TR
SV	SW SX	SY	SZ TV

1300 1200 1100 1000 900 800 700 600 500 400 300 200 100

0 100 200 300 400 500 600 700

False Origin of National Grid   Kilometres East

KEY TO ATLAS

	MOTORWAY		A ROAD
M4	Motorway with number	A1123	Other A road single/dual carriageway
S Fleet	Motorway service area	======	Road tunnel
1	Motorway junction with and without number	Toll	Toll
3	Restricted motorway junctions		Road under construction
	Motorway and junction under construction		Roundabout
	PRIMARY ROUTE		B ROAD
A3	Primary route single/dual carriageway	B2070	B road single/dual carriageway
S Grantham North	Primary route service area		B road interchange junction
BATH	Primary route destinations		B road roundabout with adjoining unclassified road
	Roundabout	→	Steep gradient
5	Distance in miles between symbols		Unclassified road single/dual carriageway
	Narrow Primary route with passing places	—o—x—	Railway station and level crossing

KEY TO ATLAS

⌂	Abbey, cathedral or priory	– – – – –	National trail
◀	Aquarium	NT	National Trust property
♖	Castle	NTS	National Trust for Scotland property
⌒	Cave	⬫	Nature reserve
♔	Country park	★	Other place of interest
♙	County cricket ground	P·R	Park and Ride location
🐂	Farm or animal centre	⚲	Picnic site
··········	Forest drive	⚙	Steam centre
✿	Garden	⛷	Ski slope natural
⚑	Golf course	⛷	Ski slope artifical
⌂	Historic house	ⓘ	Tourist Information Centre
🐎	Horse racing	☀	Viewpoint
🏁	Motor racing	ⓥ	Visitor or heritage centre
🏛	Museum	🦌	Zoological or wildlife collection
☎	AA telephone		Forest Park
⊕	Airport		Heritage coast
Ⓗ	Heliport		National Park (England & Wales)
🗼	Windmill		National Scenic Area (Scotland)

KEY TO TOURS

🚗	Tour start point	Buckland Abbey	Highlighted point of interest
➤	Direction of tour		Featured tour
▪▶▫▶	Optional detour		

KEY TO WALKS

Scale 1:25,000, 2½ inches to 1 mile, 4cm to 1 km

🚶 Start of walk		Line of walk
➡ Direction of walk	▪▪▶▪▶▪ Optional detour	
	Buckland Abbey	Highlighted point of interest

ROADS AND PATHS

M1 or A6(M)	M1 or A6(M)	Motorway
A 31(T) or A35	A 31(T) or A35	Trunk or main road
B 3074	B 3074	Secondary road
A 35	A 35	Dual carriageway
		Road generally more than 4m wide
		Road generally less than 4m wide
		Other road, drive or track
		Path

Unfenced roads and tracks are shown by pecked lines

RAILWAYS

Multiple track / Single track — Standard gauge		Embankment
		Tunnel
Narrow gauge		Road over; road under
Siding		Level crossing
Cutting		Station

PUBLIC RIGHTS OF WAY

Public rights of way may not be evident on the ground

Public paths { footpath / bridleway	++	Byway open to all traffic
Permissive path		Road used as a public path
	◆ ◆	Named path
Permissive bridleway	Pennine Way	National trail or recreational path

The representation on this map of any other road, track or path is no evidence of the existence of a right of way

RELIEF

50 ·	Heights determined by	{	Ground survey
285 ·			Air survey

Contours are at 5 and 10 metres vertical interval

SYMBOLS

▪	Place of worship { with tower / with spire, minaret or dome / without such additions	∘W, Spr	Well, Spring
			Gravel pit
▪	Building		Other pit or quarry
▪	Important building		Sand pit
. T; A; R	Telephone: public; AA; RAC		Refuse or slag heap
--□---- pylon pole	Electricity transmission line		County Boundary (England & Wales)
△ △	Triangulation pillar		Water
	Bus or coach station		Sand; sand & shingle
⏀ ⏀	Lighthouse; beacon		National Park boundary
·↑·	Site of antiquity		Mud
NT	National Trust always open		
FC	Forestry Commission		

DANGER AREA

Firing and test ranges in the area
Danger!
Observe warning notices

VEGETATION

Limits of vegetation are defined by positioning of the symbols but may be delineated also by pecks or dots

Coniferous trees		Non-coniferous trees
Orchard		Heath
Coppice		Marsh, reeds, saltings.

TOURIST AND LEISURE INFORMATION

⋏	Camp site	PC	Public convenience
𝑖	Information centre	P	Parking
𝑖	Information centre (seasonal)	☀	Viewpoint
🚐	Caravan site	⊕	Mountain rescue post
⋈	Picnic site		

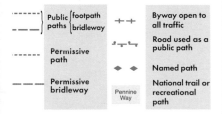

Index

A fine Swaledale landscape

Acknowledgements

Third edition verified by Outcrop Publishing Services Ltd, Cumbria

The Automobile Association wishes to thank the following photographers and libraries for their assistance in the preparation of this book

THE MANSELL COLLECTION LTD 7d
NATURE PHOTOGRAPHERS LTD 67 (R Tidman)
DAVID TARN 66, 27, 71, 73, 78a, 79, 80, 87, 95, 96, 99, 115, 116, 117, 127

All the remaining pictures, except those listed below, are held in the Association's own library (AA PHOTO LIBRARY) and were taken by David Tarn with the exception of page 10b (P Baker), 42 (J Beazley), 100 (R Eames), 11c, 97, 98 (S & O Mathews), cover, 10a, 11a, 51, 74 (J Morrison), 85 (G Rowatt).